MAKER DAD

ALSO BY MARK FRAUENFELDER

*The Computer: An Illustrated History from
Its Origins to the Present Day*

✹

*Mad Professor: Concoct Extremely
Weird Science Projects*

✹

*Made by Hand: My Adventures in the
World of Do-It-Yourself*

✹

*Rule the Web: How to Do Anything and Everything
on the Internet—Better, Faster, Easier*

MAKER DAD

DAD

LUNCH BOX GUITARS, ANTIGRAVITY JARS, AND **22** OTHER INCREDIBLY COOL **FATHER–DAUGHTER DIY PROJECTS**

Mark Frauenfelder

NEW HARVEST
HOUGHTON MIFFLIN HARCOURT
BOSTON   NEW YORK

Copyright © 2014 by Mark Frauenfelder

This edition published by special arrangement with Amazon Publishing

For information about permission to reproduce selections from this book, go to www.apub.com.

www.hmhco.com

Library of Congress Cataloging-in-Publication Data is available.
ISBN 978-0-544-11454-8

Book design by Kimberly Glyder

Printed in the United States of America
DOC 10 9 8 7 6 5

IMPORTANT NOTICE TO READERS

All do-it-yourself activities involve a degree
of risk. Skills, materials, tools, and site conditions
may vary widely. The projects in this book vary from
easy and quick to moderately challenging and challenging.
Accordingly, different projects require different skill levels,
and some may not be appropriate for all do-it-yourselfers. If you feel
uncomfortable or uncertain about undertaking a particular project, consult
or hire a professional. The author and the publisher cannot and do not assume
any responsibility for any damages, injuries, or losses as a result of following the
information in this book. Always obey local codes and laws, follow manufacturers'
operating instructions, observe safety precautions, and use common sense.

To my daughters,
Jane and Sarina.
Thank you for teaching me
so many wonderful things.
Love, Dad

CONTENTS

PROJECTS KEY

(E)   EASY AND QUICK

(M)   MODERATELY CHALLENGING

(C)   CHALLENGING. A REAL SKILL-BUILDER!

MAKER
DAD

Say Yes to Mistakes

I wasn't always an eager maker of things. I was timid about it until I became the editor of the technology project magazine *MAKE*. Working there, I met hundreds of people who made amazing things in their spare time in their garages, in their basements and backyards, and on their kitchen tables. As I got to know them, I discovered something that profoundly changed the way I thought about creativity. I learned that these "alpha makers" weren't perfect. They didn't go into their workshops and effortlessly build beautiful and functional things. Instead, they worked by trial and error. They revised their original designs, often drastically. They made plenty of mistakes and didn't get upset about it. They *expected* to make mistakes, and they learned from them. Their finished projects turned out better as a result of having made mistakes. The mistakes pointed out the problems with the project, pushing the maker to improve upon them.

This was a shock to me. One of the main reasons I didn't like to make things was because mistakes made me feel like a failure. If things didn't work out the first time, I often gave up. I know other people feel the same way. A big reason for this crippling mind-set is that we've been trained in the classroom to equate mistakes with bad grades. If our educational system teaches us one thing, it's this: "Be perfect. Avoid mistakes or you will be penalized."

Alpha makers' superpower isn't having awesome making skills, or owning a high-tech workshop filled with the latest 3-D printers and laser cutters. Their superpower is the ability to ignore the "just say no to mistakes" lesson that schools drilled into their heads from kindergarten to grad school.

When I finally learned to embrace mistakes, the world of making opened up to me. I lost my timidity and started making skateboards, musical instruments, wooden puzzles, and electronic toys. My daughters (Jane, ten, and Sarina, sixteen) joined me, and I tried my best to share with them what I learned from the alpha makers' attitude about mistakes.

When Jane, Sarina, and I made the projects for this book, we often made mistakes—drilling holes in the wrong place, splitting wood, attaching electronic components in the wrong orientation, selecting materials that didn't work the way we wanted them to, and so on. Sure, it was often frustrating, but these mistakes caused us to think about other possibilities. They sparked our imagination.

Each project in this book is the result of many iterations. It never turned out the way we expected the first time around. The second version of each project often took care of the major problems, but it was still full of annoying bugs. The third version was usually close, but not good enough. It wasn't until we built the fourth, fifth, or sixth prototype that we felt we had something worth sharing.

Even though we've tried our best to provide instructions that will ensure a successful build for you and your daughters, it's inevitable that you are going to make some mistakes along the way. Consider yourself lucky. These mistakes will give you an opportunity to be creative and resourceful, to improvise, and to come up with something even better than we did. Have fun!

We'd love to hear about your experiences making the projects in the book. Send photos and video links to markfrauenfelder@gmail.com.

MAKER DAD TOOLBOX

Most of the projects in the book can be built with tools that you probably already own. Here's a list of the tools you'll need.

- 30-watt pen-type soldering iron and rosin-core solder
- Acrylic spray
- Awl, nail, or pushpin
- Binder clips
- Clamps (spring or woodworking)
- Computer and printer
- Coping saw
- Craft knife
- Cutting pad
- Digital Camera
- Drill press or hand drill and various bits
- Electric whisk
- Hammer
- Hand saw or pocket saw
- Hot glue gun and hot glue sticks
- Metal or plastic ruler
- Microwave oven
- Needle-nose pliers
- Paintbrushes and acrylic paints
- Polyurethane spray
- Rat-tail file
- Rotary cutting tool, such as a Dremel
- Sandpaper, various grits
- Scissors
- Screwdrivers (flat-head and Phillips-head)
- Scroll saw or band saw
- Solder sucker or a spool of desoldering wick
- Surform Shaver
- Tape, clear and masking
- Wire cutters
- Wire strippers
- Wood glue

ANTIGRAVITY JAR

How would you like to be able to turn off gravity anytime you feel like it? Just imagine, you could drift above the sidewalk or move heavy things without breaking a sweat. Antigravity technology has been a favorite science fiction fantasy since before H. G. Wells introduced a floating metal called "cavorite" in his 1901 novel, *The First Men in the Moon*. But in the real world, antigravity technology has remained elusive. The most promising research in anti-gravity has come from Russia. In 1992, a Russian physicist named Evgeny Podkletnov presented an article in a scientific journal called *Physica C* in which he reported that he had built a gravity shield out of a magnet and a supercon-ductor. Objects under the influence of the shield, he wrote, weighed 0.3 percent less. NASA has spent hundreds of thousands of dollars trying to duplicate Podkletnov's device without success. In recent years, Podkletnov has teamed up with an Italian physicist named Giovanni Modanese to make a "gravity repulsion beam" that observers claim can move a pendulum located 150 meters from the device.

Our antigravity project is just a magic trick, but you can have a lot of fun fooling your friends into believing that you own a small bottle of invisible antigravity fluid that can make a paper clip float inside a jar. I first came across this trick when I was a kid, and I have never forgotten my sur-prise and delight when I saw the paper clip floating like a helium balloon tied to a string.

THINGS YOU NEED TO MAKE AN ANTIGRAVITY JAR

MATERIALS

- **Clear tape,** to attach the thread to the bottom of the jar
- **Thread,** one that is as thin as possible
- **Metal paper clip.** A brightly colored one is best because it's easier to see than a bare metal paper clip.
- **Glass jar with a lid.** We used a Trader Joe's coconut oil jar, but any glass jar will do, such as a peanut butter or spaghetti sauce jar.
- **Neodymium magnet.** We used a ½-inch cube magnet. Neodymium magnets of this size cost about $10 per pack of four. We bought ours online. You can also pick them up at a hobby store.

The stronger the magnet the better, but please note that neodymium magnets are strong and can easily pinch your fingers, so be careful when handling them.

- **Flat black spray paint (optional),** to make the magnet harder to see
- **Tiny jar or bottle,** to hold the invisible antigravity fluid. A small jar with an eyedropper is ideal if you have one.

TOOLS

- **Scissors**

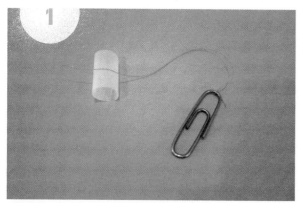

How to Make the Antigravity Jar

1 **Attach tape and thread to the paper clip.** Use the scissors to cut about 6 inches of thread (more or less, depending on the size of the jar). Tie one end securely to the paper clip. Attach the other end to a small loop of tape. Make sure an inch or so of the thread hangs off the tape loop, because this will come in handy when you are adjusting the length of the thread.

2 **Secure the tape loop to the bottom of the jar.** Use a pen or a chopstick to stick the tape against the inside of the bottom of the jar. Position the tape loop so that the long end of the thread is at the center of the jar bottom.

3 **Place the magnet on the inside of the jar lid.** If the lid is made of magnetic metal, just stick it right on. If not, use tape. Make sure the magnet's orientation is correct for the paper clip—it should exert a strong pull on the paper clip toward the center of the magnet's exposed face. If it pulls the paper clip to the side or repels it, turn the magnet so that another face is exposed. Keep trying until you get a nice strong tug on the paper clip.

Optional: If you have some flat black spray paint, you can make it very difficult for your friends to spot the magnet by painting the inside of the lid and the magnet black. This is a commonly used technique in magic tricks. Flat black is very hard to see. Glossy black paint reflects light, so it's not as good for the purposes of this project.

4   **Adjust the string length.** Before screwing the lid on, hang the jar upside down. If the paper clip extends past the mouth of the jar, it's too long. Adjust the length by carefully pulling on the short end of the thread with the needle-nose pliers until the paper clip is about 1.5 inches below the mouth of the jar. You may need to lightly push against the tape loop with your pen or chopstick while you are pulling on the string so that the tape doesn't come loose. Now, screw the lid on, tip the jar upside down, and then slowly tip it upright. Is the paper clip suspended like a balloon on a string? If so, good! If not, the string is too short and you'll have to repeat this step until you get the length you need.

Now it's time to show your creation!

How to Perform the Magic Trick

1   Start with the paper clip lying at the bottom of the sealed jar.

2   Show the tiny jar or bottle and say, "Have you heard that NASA has invented a fluid that cancels the effects of gravity? We have a friend that works at NASA and she gave us a small jar of the stuff."

3   Unscrew the lid of the jar with the paper clip and set it down, being careful not to reveal the magnet attached to the lid. Then slowly and carefully open the tiny jar or bottle as if it contains something very precious. Pretend to pour (or squeeze from the dropper) a bit of the invisible fluid into the jar with the paper clip. Say, "You only need a drop for it to work." Recap the small jar or bottle, then screw the lid on to the jar with the paper clip.

4   Say, "I need to mix the fluid in the jar." Tip the jar over so the paper clip engages with the magnet. Then slowly tip the jar upright. The paper clip will wobble and rotate on the thread, which heightens the effect that unseen antigravity forces are at work.

5   After a few seconds, say, "When you let the antigravity fluid escape from the jar, the paper clip will fall." Unscrew the lid and tip the lid up as if you are allowing the fluid to leak out of the jar. Of course, what you are really doing is moving the magnet away from the paper clip, causing it to drop.

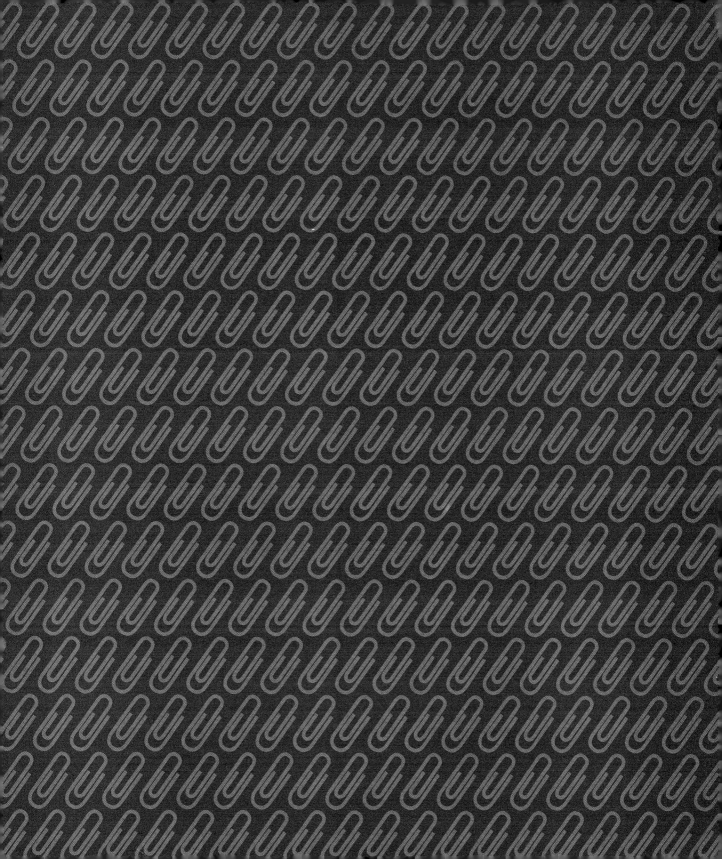

DRAWBOT

A lively gadget that draws circular patterns by itself

When I was young, my sister and I were fanatically devoted to a public television show called *Zoom,* which ran from 1972 to 1978. Each episode featured activities and fun projects to make. One of them was a drawing robot made from a motor, felt-tip pens, and a paper cup. You could set it down on a large sheet of paper, switch on the motor, and watch it draw colorful spirograph-style abstract art. The drawbot presented here—made from scrap wood, coat hanger wire, binder clips, a toy motor, and felt-tip pens—is more durable than the *Zoom* drawbot, and you can easily adjust the angles of the pens to change the patterns it draws.

THINGS YOU NEED TO MAKE A DRAWBOT

MATERIALS

- **Plywood or board**, 4½ in. × 4½ in. × ³⁄₁₆ in.
- **3 wood blocks**, ¾ in. × ¾ in. × 2½ in.
- **Wood glue**
- **Ball-point pen ink tube**
- **1.5-volt hobby DC motor**
- **Superglue**
- **Wire hanger**
- **Craft pom-pom**
- **Wooden dowel**, ¼-inch diameter
- **2 cable ties**
- **AA battery holder**
- **2 wood screws**, ¼ inch long
- **3 wood screws**, ½ inch long
- **3 metal washers**, ⅝ inch (outer diameter)
- **3 binder clips**, 1¼ in. × ¾ in.
- **3 felt-tip pens**
- **AA battery**

TOOLS

- **Computer and printer**
- **Scissors**
- **Pencil**
- **Pushpin**
- **Scroll saw, band saw, or coping saw**
- **Drill with bits**
- **Clamps**
- **Wire cutters**
- **Needle-nose pliers**
- **30-watt pen-type soldering iron and rosin-core solder.** Available for about $10 online.
- **Solder sucker or a spool of desoldering wick,** so you can remove solder easily
- **Screwdriver**

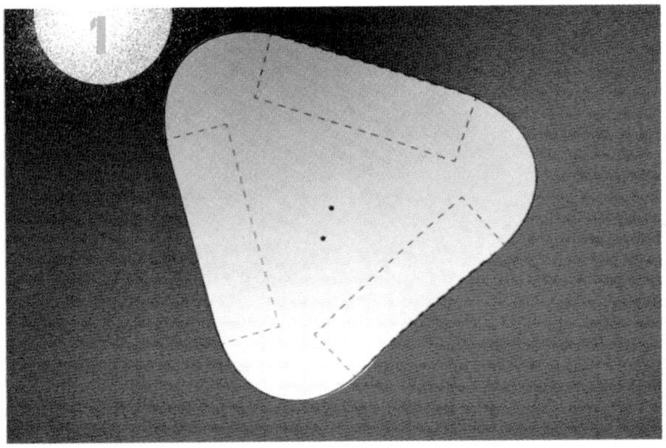
1

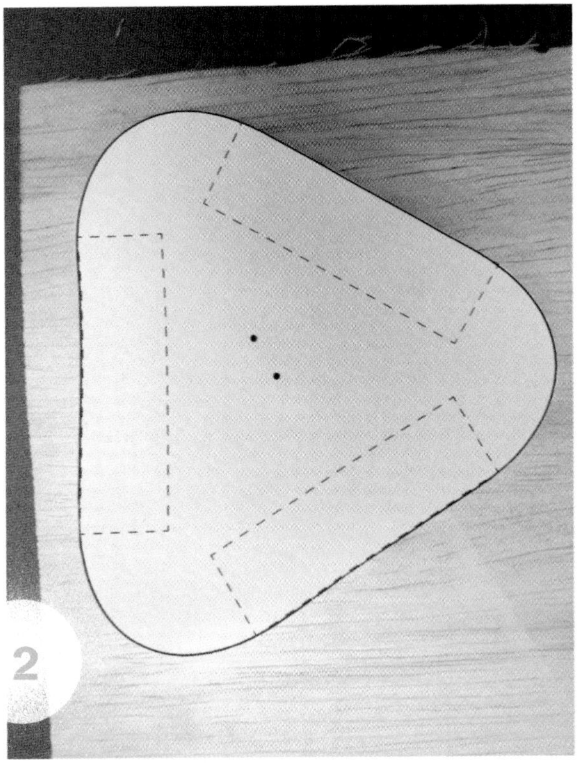
2

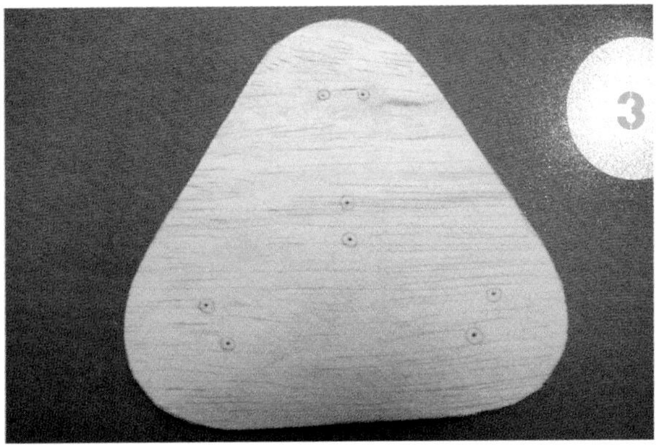
3

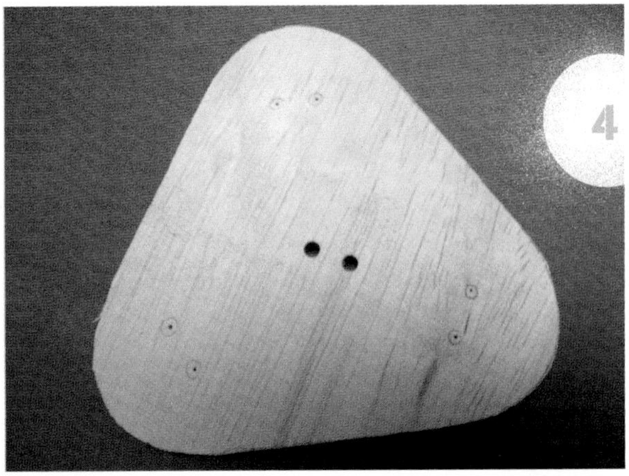
4

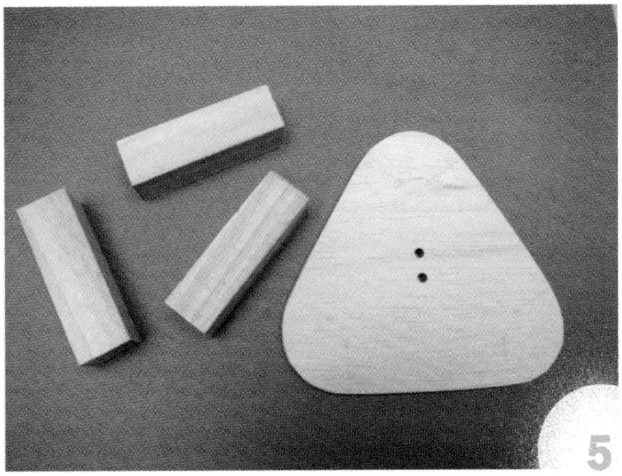
5

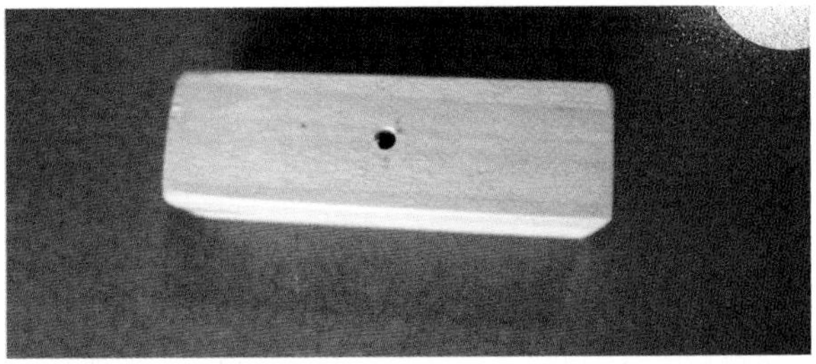

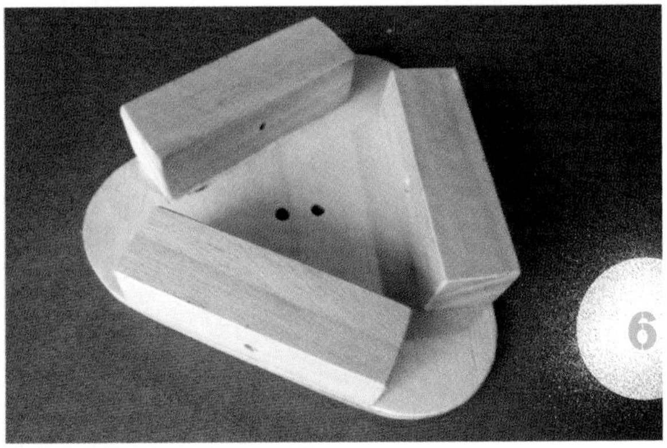
6

How to Make a Drawbot

1 **Print out the template for the drawbot.** You can download the PDF from makerdad.org. Once you've printed it out, carefully cut it out with scissors.

2 **Transfer the template shape to the plywood.** Draw along the edge of the paper with a pencil. Also, use a pushpin to mark the two holes near the center, as well as the corners of the dotted line rectangles. This will help you position the wood blocks when you glue them on later.

3 **Cut out the triangle shape.** This is easy with a powered band saw or a scroll saw. If you don't have either, use a coping saw. It will take a bit longer, but it will look great if you take your time.

4 **Drill the two holes in the triangle shape.** A ³⁄₁₆-inch bit will do the trick.

5 **Drill holes through the wood blocks.** We used a ⅛-inch bit, but you should use a bit size that's slightly smaller than the thread diameter of your screws. Each block gets one hole drilled in the middle of a face of the block as shown.

6 **Glue the blocks to the triangle shape.** Make sure not to glue the faces with the holes. Clamp the blocks down and let them dry for about a half hour before working with these pieces again. While the glue is drying, you can work on the next steps.

7 **Cut off the end of a ball-point pen ink tube.** About ½ to ¾ inch long is sufficient. Make sure the part you snip off doesn't have any ink in it or it will get all over everything and make a mess.

8 **Attach the ink tube to the motor's shaft.** It should fit snugly. If not, secure it with a drop of superglue.

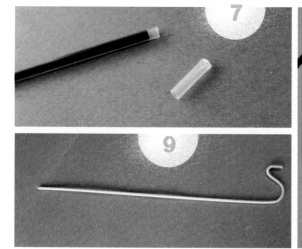

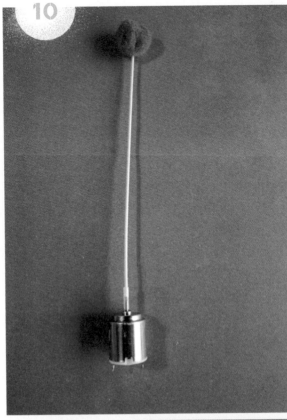

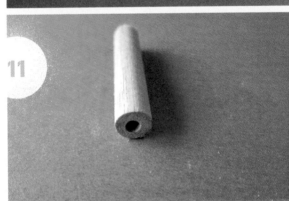

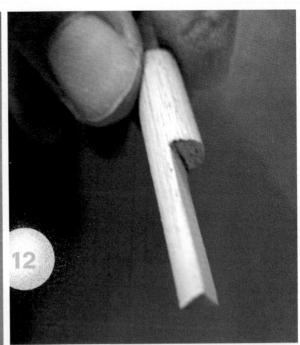

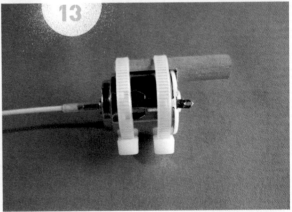

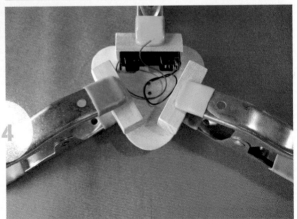

9   **Cut an 8-inch length of wire from a coat hanger with the wire cutters.** It's okay to keep the curvy part at the end as shown.

10 **Attach a craft pom-pom to the end of the coat hanger.** Make a U shape at the end of the coat hanger, slide the pom-pom in the U, and pinch it shut with the pliers. You should not be able to feel any sharp ends. Stick the other end of the coat hanger wire into the ink tube.

11 **Cut the dowel to 2¼ inches long.** Then drill a hole into it lengthwise. The hole should be slightly longer than the ¼-inch-long wood screw you are using, and the hole's diameter should be slightly less than the screw's thread diameter.

12 **Cut the dowel to form a flat face.** We removed a ⅞-inch-long semicylinder from the dowel as shown. You might need to remove more or less, depending on the size of the motor you are using.

13 **Mount the motor to the dowel.** Use two cable ties to secure the motor to the dowel. Trim the ends of the cable ties. Solder the battery holder leads to the motor. Use the screwdriver to attach the dowel to the triangle with a wood screw. Be careful when tightening, because the dowel could split if you overtighten the screw.

14 **Attach the battery holder.** Use a ¼-inch-long screw with a low-profile head to attach the battery pack to one of the wood blocks as shown. We kept the clamps on during this step to make sure we didn't knock the blocks loose from the triangle shape before the glue had set.

    Note: If your battery pack has an on/off switch, make sure it's accessible.

15 **Attach the binder clips.** Use a wood screw and a washer for each binder clip. Slide the clip as far as possible to the left and tighten the screw.

15

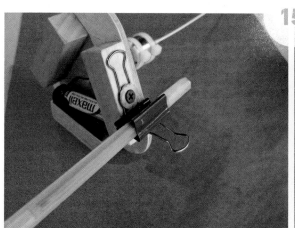
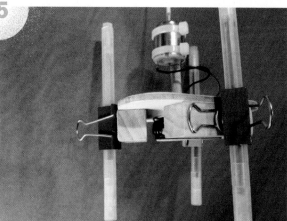

16   **Clamp three felt-tip pens in the binder clips.** Your completed drawbot should look like this. You are now ready to start drawing!

17   **Test your drawbot.** Insert a battery, remove the pen caps, and set the drawbot on a large piece of paper.

Now, watch it draw!

Tips

If your battery pack doesn't have a switch, you can either pull out the battery or insert a thin strip of plastic between the battery and the contact inside the battery holder. We use a bread bag clip.

If the drawbot looks like it is about to move off the piece of paper or gets stuck spinning in the same spot for a while, you can either pick it up while it is still running or gently lift the edge of the paper to direct the drawbot to a different spot.

To change the "personality" of the drawbot you can slightly bend the coat hanger wire, or try using a longer or shorter piece of coat hanger wire. You can also adjust the angle of the binder clips by rotating them.

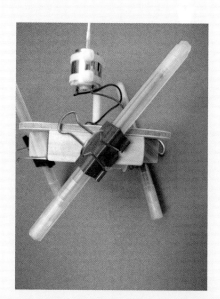

LONGBOARD

Smooth-riding skateboard with a bouncy curve

A couple of years ago, when Sarina was thirteen, she asked for a skateboard. I gave her my twenty-year-old board (which wasn't seeing much use). She liked to ride it along the bank of the Los Angeles River, and I would ride with her on a Razor scooter. But after a while, I started to miss having a skateboard, and I thought it would be fun to make one. I put it off for a few months, until I saw a video of Lloyd Kahn, the well-known maker and Shelter Publications guru, cruising down a gently sloped street (see video at makerdad.org). He was seventy-six years old at the time, and his skating skills are top-notch. This was the inspiration I needed to get off my butt and make my own longboard. I went online to look for plans. There are many plans and kits available, but they seemed overly complex for what I was setting out to do. I simply wanted a four-foot-long board that wouldn't sag too much when I stood in the middle of it. My solution was to make a board with a hump in it.

MATERIALS

- **Wood for board.** You can use two pieces of ¼ in. × 7¼ in. × 4 ft. poplar hobby board (available at Home Depot or online at denoon.com). You can also use ⅛- or ¼-inch-thick Baltic birch plywood (make sure it is Baltic birch, not just plain old birch, which is too weak). Baltic birch is available at woodcraft.com.

- **Wood glue,** such as Gorilla Wood Glue or Titebond III

- **Polyurethane spray,** to make the wood water-resistant

- **Acrylic paints and paintbrushes**

- **Skate trucks and wheels.** I ordered a set of 6-inch-wide longboard trucks and 76 mm diameter wheels online for about $35.

- **Grip tape,** to apply to the skateboard deck. Available from skate shops or online.

TOOLS

- **Band saw, jigsaw, or handsaw and folding pocket saw**

- **Drop cloth**

- **Paintbrush,** for glue

- **2 bricks,** to suspend the board while the glue dries

- **Something heavy,** like a 40-pound bag of kitty litter, a 5-gallon bucket filled with water, or a box of books

- **6 or more spring clamps,** to clamp the glued boards together

- **Computer and printer**

- **Scissors**

- **Clear tape**

- **Pencil**

- **Pushpin**

- **Drill and bits**

- **Sandpaper,** various grits

- **Skateboard tool (optional, but handy).** Otherwise a Phillips-head screwdriver or socket set.

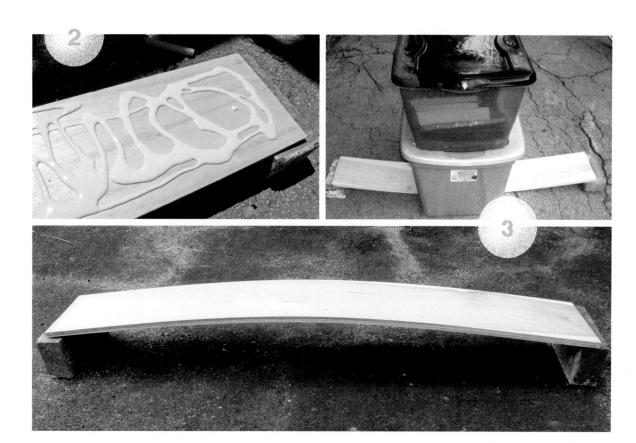

How to Make a Longboard

1. **Cut the boards to rough size.** We found ¼-inch-thick poplar hobby boards at Home Depot, which were the perfect size for a 4-foot-long skateboard: 7¼ inches wide and 4 feet long. If you have wider and longer sheets, cut them to size with a jigsaw, band saw, or handsaw. If you are using ¼-inch-thick plywood, then you need two sheets of wood. If you are using ⅛-inch-thick Baltic birch, you can probably get away with using three sheets for lightweight riders and four sheets for heavier riders.

2. **Glue the boards together.** Use a drop cloth to keep glue from dripping on the floor (unless you are outdoors and don't care about glue drips). Apply a generous amount of glue to the sides of the boards that will be stuck together. Use the paintbrush to spread the glue evenly. Press the two sticky sides together and make sure the boards are aligned.

3. **Suspend the boards between two bricks placed at its far ends.** We set a couple of heavy boxes of books in the middle of the board so that it sagged in a U shape. Then pinch the boards together with clamps. This will cause some glue to be squeezed out from between the boards, which is why you might want a drop cloth. Do not disturb the setup for 24 hours. When you remove the weight, the boards will remain warped, which is what you want. Test it out by flipping the boards over, standing on the hump, and bouncing up and down a bunch of times to make sure it can support your weight without breaking.

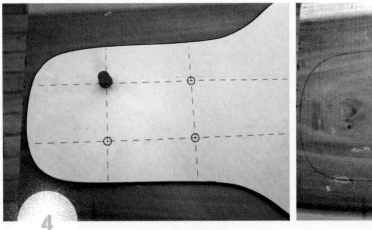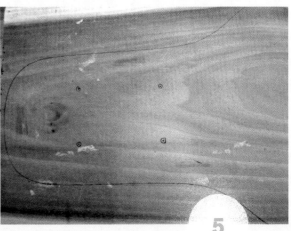

4 Cut the ends of the deck. Next, you need to make a cutting pattern for the ends of the skateboard. It helps if you have photos of skateboards on hand for reference (use Google Images and search for "longboard"). We drew a cutting pattern template using Adobe Illustrator. You can download it from makerdad.org. Print out the template, cut it out with scissors, and tape it to one end of your new board. Use a pencil to transfer the outline to the board. We used the same template on both ends. We also marked the place to drill the truck bolt holes with a pushpin. With a jigsaw, band saw, or pocket saw, cut along the pencil line. It's better to cut a little outside the pencil line than inside the pencil line because it's easy to use sandpaper on the deck to perfect the shape.

5 Drill the holes for the trucks. Most longboard trucks have bolt hole patterns that are 1⅝ inches wide and 2½ inches tall. If you are using the template we have at makerdad.org, you can easily position the truck hole pattern and then drill holes through the deck with a ³⁄₁₆-inch drill bit. Be careful with this step, because if your hole patterns are misaligned you'll have to scrap the deck and start over.

6 Sand the deck. Use various grits of sandpaper to smooth out all the edges and surfaces.

7 Seal the deck. Spray several coats of aerosol polyurethane on the deck. Between each coat, let the polyurethane spray dry and sand it lightly with fine-grit sandpaper.

8 Paint the deck. Use acrylic paint to paint your design on the underside of the board. You can also paint the top, but the design will be mostly covered by the grip tape that you will apply to the top in the final step. After you're done, give the painted board a couple additional coats of polyurethane.

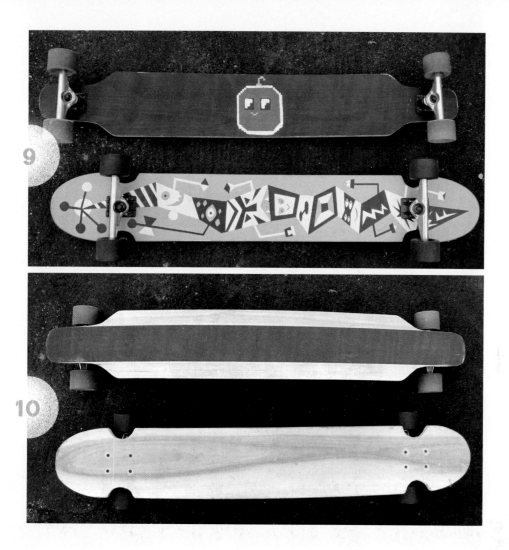

9 **Add the trucks and wheels.** Make sure the trucks are oriented so that the rubber plugs are facing the middle of the skateboard deck. Don't put them on the other way around or you will be surprised when you try to ride it and discover that it turns in the opposite direction you want it to go! The part of the truck with the nut should be toward the center of the board, as shown in the above step. A skateboard tool comes in handy when adjusting and installing the wheels and trucks. Adjust the trucks so that you can turn easily when you lean from side to side. Don't make them so loose that the board is wobbly, though.

10 **Apply grip tape to the top of the deck.** Grip tape is important because it will keep your shoes from sliding off the board. In the image above, the board on top has a 3¾-inch strip of grip tape running down the length of the deck. The board on the bottom is completely covered with clear grip tape. *Now your skateboard is ready to ride!* Be sure to ride in a safe area and wear safety gear, such as a helmet, kneepads, elbow pads, and wrist protectors.

MID-CENTURY ROCKING CHAIR

Comfy furniture for reading, gaming, or chilling

My daughters and I wanted to make something to sit on that was comfortable and low to the ground like a beanbag chair, but that was also more fun, like a rocking chair. It also had to be easy to make. We searched on Google and came across a photo of a chair built around 1950 by Alexey Brodovitch, a designer who was the art director at *Harper's Bazaar* from 1934 to 1958. The chair had a fun shape and looked fairly simple to build. Using the photo as a reference, we built a similar chair out of plywood and dowels. We discovered that the chair was not very sturdy. We changed the design to have better support, and a few iterations later we came up with a chair that feels more robust. Jane and Sarina love to sit in this chair and read or use their iPhones.

THINGS YOU NEED TO MAKE A MID–CENTURY ROCKING CHAIR

MATERIALS

- **One 4 ft. × 2 ft. plywood panel.** We used ½-inch-thick plywood, which worked well for my daughters' weight (under 110 pounds). I weigh 165 and sat in it without fear that it would collapse. If you weigh more than me I recommend going with ¾-inch-thick plywood.

- **2 pieces of wood,** ¾ in. × ¾ in. × 8 in.

- **Wood glue**

- **Acrylic spray paint**

- **Urethane spray sealer**

- **3 wood dowels,** 24 inches long and 1 inch or more in diameter

- **6 flat-head Phillips wood screws,** 2 inches long

- **4 flat-head Phillips wood screws,** 1 inch long

- **6 metal washers,** 1-inch outer diameter, ¼-inch inner diameter

- **4 metal washers,** ½-inch outer diameter, ¼-inch inner diameter

- **Strong rope or cord,** 100 feet. For one chair we used ⅜-inch poly rope. For another chair we used ¼-inch diameter Ethernet cable.

TOOLS

- **Computer and printer**
- **Craft knife**
- **Metal or plastic ruler,** for cutting paper along a straight line
- **Cutting surface,** such as a self-healing cutting mat
- **Scissors**
- **Clear tape**
- **Pencil**
- **Awl, nail, or pushpin**
- **Band saw, jigsaw, or pocket saw**
- **Spring clamps**
- **Sandpaper,** various grits
- **Drill with various bits**
- **Hammer**

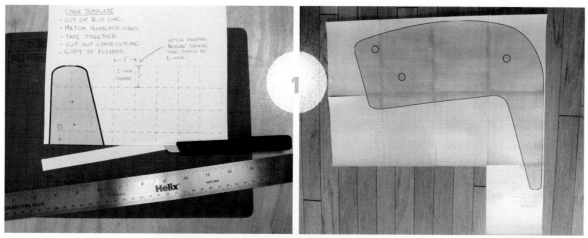

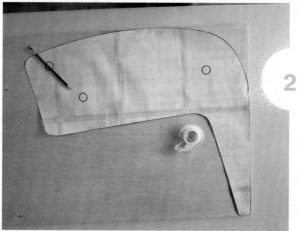

How to Make a Mid-Century Rocking Chair

1 **Print out the chair template.** The first thing you need to do is make a full-sized template that you will attach to the plywood so you can mark out the shape of the chair. Download the nine-page chair template document from makerdad.org and print it out. (The squares of the dotted line grid should measure 1 inch on each side. If they don't, adjust your printer settings and try again.)

2 **Assemble the template.** Using a craft knife and ruler on a safe cutting surface, cut each sheet of paper along the blue lines and match the numbered sides. Tape the sheets together. Use scissors to cut the outline of the chair.

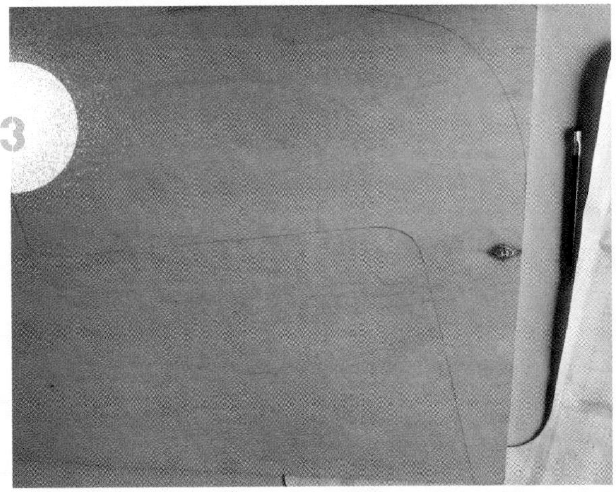

3

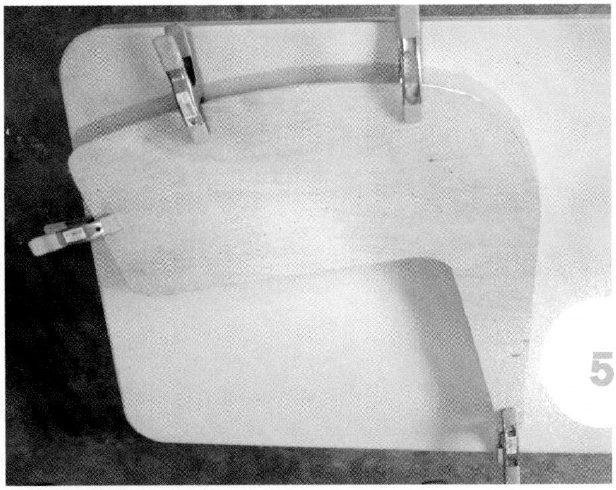

5

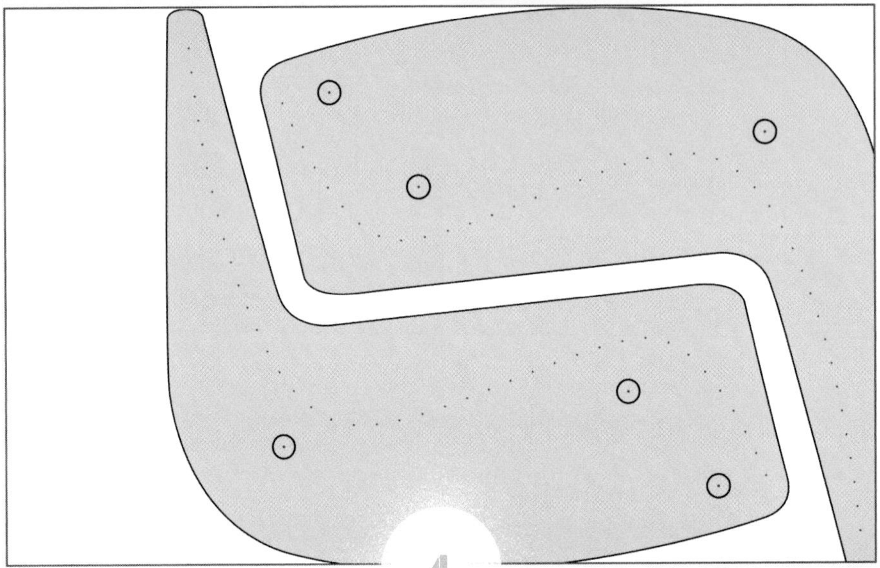

4

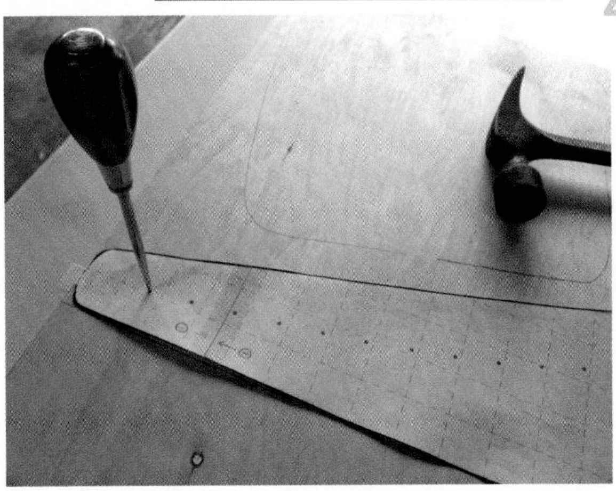

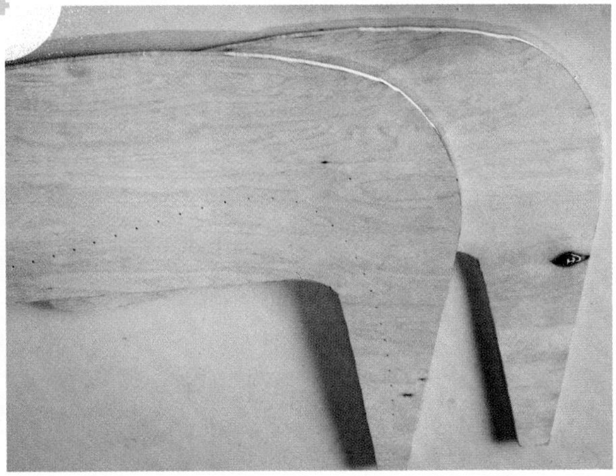

3 **Transfer the template shape to the plywood.** Align the back of the chair shape along the short end of the plywood. Make sure that the paper doesn't hang over the edge of the plywood anywhere. Tack down the template with a few pieces of tape. With a pencil, carefully trace the outline of the template on the plywood.

4 **Make another chair outline on the plywood.** Remove the template and rotate it 180 degrees. Move it close to the first outline you drew, as shown. Trace around the template with a pencil as before. But this time you are going to mark drill holes before taking the paper off. Use an awl, nail, or pushpin to punch a hole through the red circles into the plywood. You don't need to make a deep hole, just big enough to see where to drill later on. Now you can remove the template. Save it for reference and for building other chairs.

5 **Prepare the chair shapes.** Use a band saw, pocket saw, or jigsaw to cut out the chair shapes. Watch out for splinters! Clamp the two pieces together with the drill holes exposed. Use sandpaper to shape and smooth the edges down so they match. Keep the sides clamped together to drill the holes. Use a ¼-inch drill bit to drill the five green holes for the dowels and brace. For the forty grey holes, use a drill bit that's ⅛ inch larger than the diameter of the rope or cord you are using. For instance, if you are using ¼-inch diameter cord, use a ⅜-inch drill bit. Drill all the holes completely through each side of the wood.

6 **Prepare the stability brace.** Cut an 8 in. × 24 in. rectangle from the plywood panel. Drill ⁷⁄₆₄-inch holes 7¼ inches apart through the sides of both ends of the ¾ in. × ¾ in. pieces of wood as shown. Glue and clamp the ¾ in. × ¾ in. pieces to the ends of the rectangular piece of plywood and let dry for about 30 minutes. While you are waiting for the glue to dry, you can move on to steps 7 and 8.

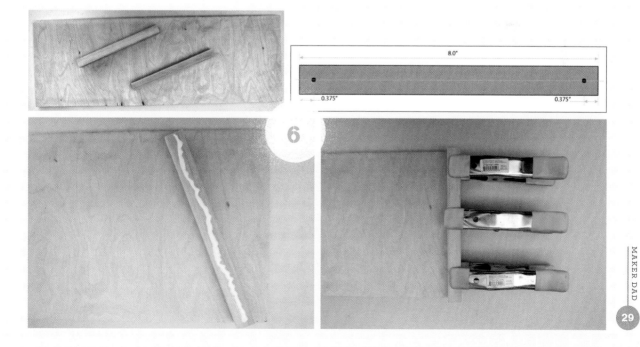

7 **Paint the chair sides.** We used red acrylic spray paint and painted about three coats of paint on each side of both chair pieces. One can was enough for two chairs. When the brace has dried for about 30 minutes, you can remove the clamps and paint it, too. We added a coat of urethane spray sealer for a glossy finish.

8 **Prepare the dowels.** Cut the three dowels to 24 inches long (you can go up to 28 inches, but any longer than that and you'll need a longer piece of rope or cord). Drill 1-inch-deep holes down the centers of each end with a $\frac{7}{64}$-inch bit.

9 **Assemble the chair.** Attach the dowels and brace to the chair sides with the screws. Use metal washers as shown.

10 **Weave the cord or rope through the holes.** Starting with a hole on the bottom, run your rope or cord through the holes as if you were lacing a shoe. It's a bit tricky getting the rope to remain tight. Do the best you can. Tie a knot in the rope on the inside of the hole you started from to keep the cord taut.

11 **Tighten the rope or cord.** First, sit in the chair for a while to stretch out the rope. Then, starting from the bottom length of rope, pull from the middle to take up the slack and work your way up, one "rung" at a time. If you want to get the rope even tighter, use the claw end of a hammer to stretch it through the holes. Put a piece of cloth under the hammer so you don't mar the wood. Be careful about pulling the rope too hard or you could break it. Pinch the rope against the hole as you pull the rope through the hole above it. Work your way up to the top. You may have to do this a few times until the rope is tight enough.

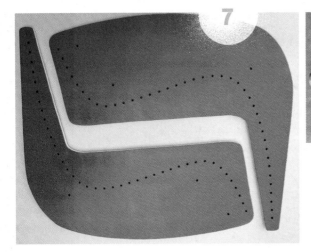

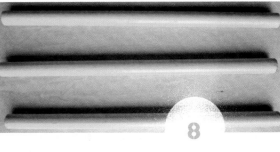

SOAP SHAPES

Create small sculptures that keep your hands clean

For Father's Day, my wife and daughters took me to one of my favorite places in Los Angeles: Abbot Kinney Boulevard in Venice, California. I like the many one-of-a-kind shops there with handmade goods for sale. Our last visit was the inspiration for this project. In one store my daughters found a dish filled with soap in the shape of baby doll hands. They were weird and appealing at the same time. They also looked like something that would be fun to make at home. We'd never cast soap before, but I remembered seeing blocks of glycerin soap at a hobby shop. We already had some silicone molding compound (purchased at the same hobby store) that we could use to make molds. A few days later my daughters and I were making molds of our toes, fingers, and various toys, and casting colorful pieces of soap from them.

This is one of the easiest projects in the book, and girls of all ages will have fun making their own soap in unique shapes and colors.

MATERIALS

- **Objects to use as your mold original.**
Many kinds of small objects can be
used to make your molds. My kids like
using their own fingers and toes as well
as toys. Select squat objects without
long or flat extremities. Thin parts will
give you problems—a toy octopus with
slender arms is likely to result in a soap
casting that breaks when you remove it
from the mold. Orientation in the putty is
important, too. Take a look at the objects
shown here. The foot should have the
sole facing up in the putty, and the hand
should have the wrist facing up. This will
make it easier to remove the soap after it
hardens in the mold.

- **Silicone molding putty.** It comes in two
parts, which you need to mix together. The
most popular brand is EasyMold Silicone
Putty and is available at hobby stores and
online.

- **Soap base.** Buy a pound or two of
microwavable soap base. Most hobby
stores carry it, and it's easy to order online
(usually under $5 per pound). We used
the basic clear glycerin soap, but you can
use any soap base that you can melt in a
microwave and pour into a mold. To see
the variety of soap bases available, visit
bulkapothecary.com. (We tried melting
regular bar soap, but it didn't melt—
it just puffed up and became crusty.)

- **Soap dye.** We were tempted to use
ordinary food coloring to tint our soap,
but food coloring can stain fabric.
So instead, we paid a few dollars and
bought specially made soap dye.

- **Scents (optional).** We didn't buy
fragrances to make our soap, but hobby
shops sell a variety of scents, such as
peppermint and cinnamon.

TOOLS

- **Knife**
- **Cutting board**
- **Pyrex measuring cup**
- **Microwave oven**
- **Spoon**

How to Make Soap Shapes

1   **Select your mold original.** Small, squat objects will give you better castings. This small plastic owl is the perfect shape for making a mold, because there are no long, thin parts. The silicone molding putty had no problem picking up the object's texture, either.

2   **Prepare the silicone putty.** Take equal amounts of putty from each of the two containers. They don't have to be exact, but they should be close. Don't use more putty than you need (it's about $15 per half pound). A thin-walled mold will work just as well as a thicker (and more costly) mold.

3   **Mix the putty.** Knead the two putties together until they are completely blended and the putty is a uniform color. The putty cures fast, so as soon as it's mixed, move to the next step.

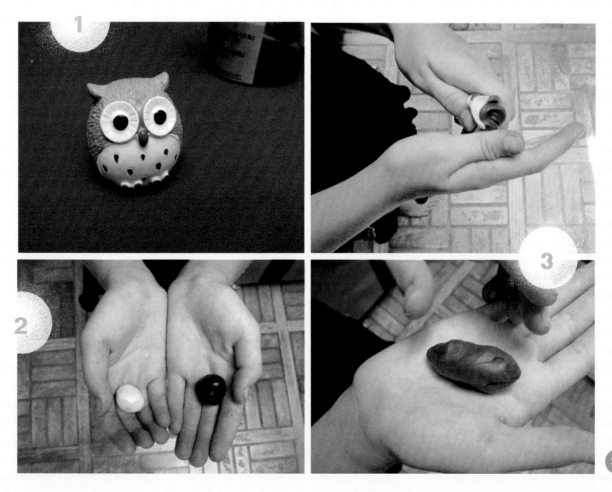

4   **Make the mold.** Start forming the putty over the object. Work quickly, because the putty starts curing immediately. You have about 1 minute to completely cover the object with putty before the putty becomes unworkable. Be sure to leave a large opening in the mold so you'll have a place to pour the melted soap (and to remove the soap after it has hardened). In the case of the owl, we left the bottom uncovered.

5   **Allow the putty to cure.** While we waited 25 minutes for the silicone putty on Jane's owl to cure, we made a mold of my thumb.

6   **Remove the objects from the molds.** It was easy to pull my thumb from the mold because it had gotten sweaty after wearing the silicone mold for 25 minutes and slid right out. Jane had no trouble popping the owl out of the mold. She held the mold in one hand, pushed on the owl's head with her finger, and the piece came out. Resist the temptation to peel the silicone off the object, because it might tear.

7   **Melt the soap.** Use a knife and a cutting board to chop a small block of the soap base into cubes. Put the cubes into a Pyrex measuring cup and microwave for 15 seconds. Check to see if the cubes have melted completely. If not, put them in the microwave for another 5 seconds and repeat until melted. You want to be careful not to burn the soap because it will give off an unpleasant odor. Nobody likes stinky soap!

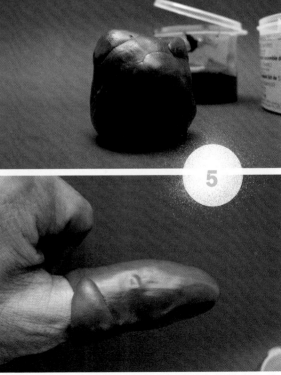

8   **Mix in the soap dye.** Add a drop or two of the soap dye and stir it with a spoon. If the soap starts to coagulate, give it another 5 or 10 seconds in the microwave.

Optional: Add a few drops of the scent of your choice and stir it in.

9   **Pour the melted soap into the molds.** We propped up the molds in espresso cups before pouring in the melted soap. When you are finished pouring, set the molds in a place where they won't be disturbed for an hour or so.

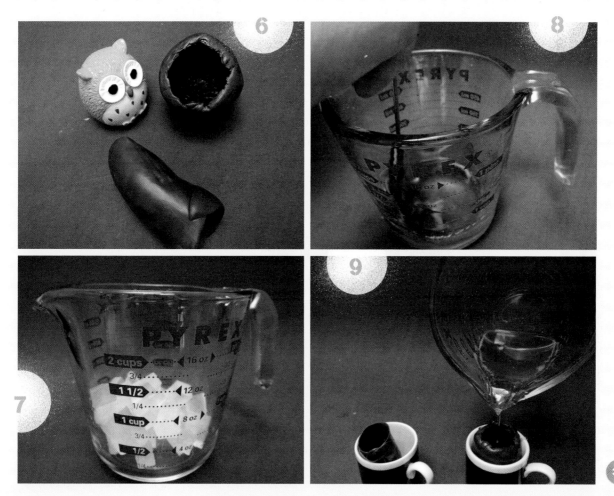

10 **Remove the soap from the molds.** When the soap has hardened you can push it out of the mold. Jane remarked that making soap is like making pancakes, because the first ones usually aren't as good as subsequent ones. I agree. The first time you use a silicone mold, the soap will probably have a lot of unsightly surface bubbles (like the one shown here). Fortunately, you can simply remelt and repour the soap. We've also found that rubbing a drop of olive oil around the inside surface of the mold will reduce the bubbles.

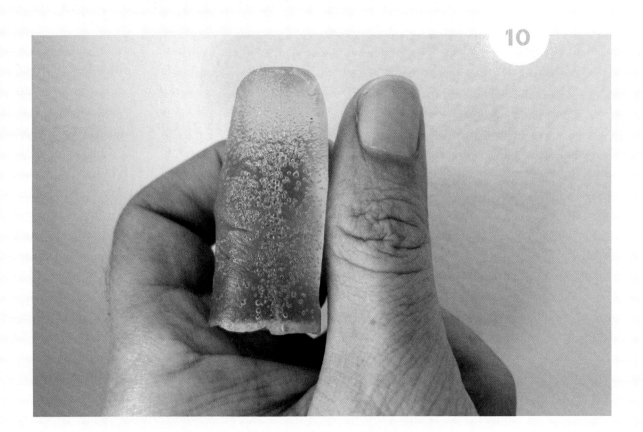

10

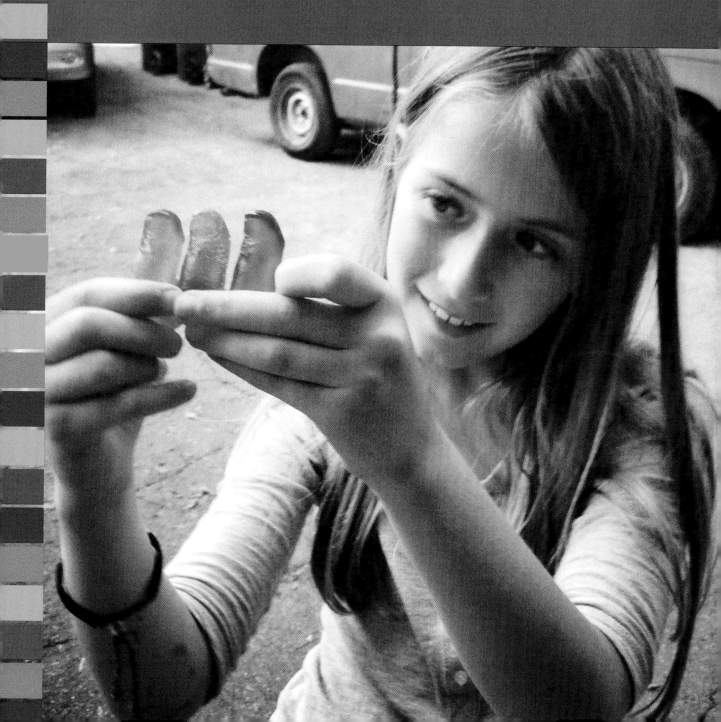

Jane's Finger Collection

Jane has become obsessed with making soap casts of her thumb! Here are a few of the pieces of thumb soap she's made. We'd love to see photos of your soap shapes. E-mail them to markfrauenfelder@gmail.com.

GIANT BUBBLES

Make monster-sized soap bubbles

Have you ever seen people making giant bubbles on the beach? They use a special wand made from two sticks that are attached to a thick, absorbent wick that holds plenty of bubble solution. You can build the same kind of wand at home from an old T-shirt and other inexpensive materials.

THINGS YOU NEED TO MAKE A GIANT BUBBLE WAND

MATERIALS

- **Old cotton T-shirt.** This is the wick that holds the bubble solution. Use 100 percent cotton for the best results.
- **String,** to tie the T-shirt to the sticks
- **2 sticks.** These can be dowels, broom-sticks, bamboo, or any other long stick-like things. We used two 28-inch wood dowels that were ⅜ inch in diameter.

- **1 large metal washer,** to weigh down the T-shirt wick; 2 small washers or a metal nut works as well.
- **Bubble solution.** We used a solution called Super Miracle Bubbles. It cost $5 for a 64-ounce bottle at Big 5 Sporting Goods. Lots of websites have bubble-solution-making recipes if you want to experiment.
- **Plastic bucket or large bowl,** to hold the bubble solution

TOOLS

- **Scissors,** to cut the T-shirt and the string
- **File or drill and bit (optional),** to make a hole in the sticks for the string

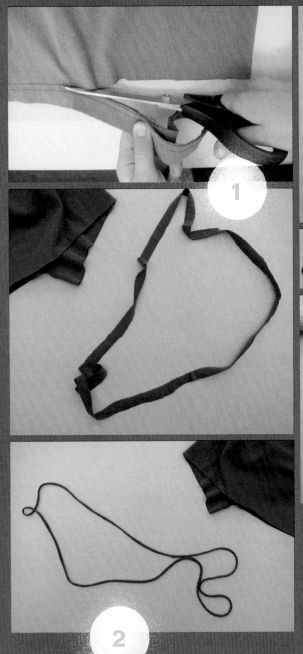

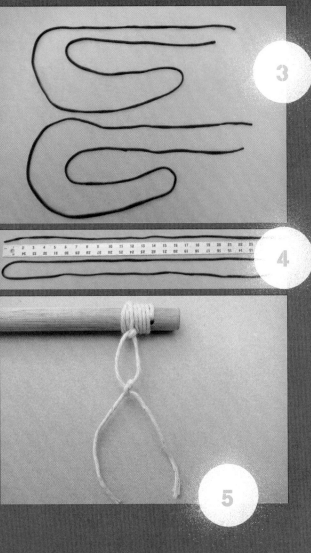

How to Make a Giant Bubble Wand

1 **Cut a ½-inch-wide strip from the cotton T-shirt.** With the scissors, cut off the hem around the bottom of the shirt and discard it. Then cut a ½-inch-wide loop from the bottom of the shirt.

2 **Stretch the T-shirt loop.** When you release it, the fabric will roll up and it will look like a rope.

3 **Make another loop.** Repeat steps 1 and 2 above. Then snip the loops so you have two long strips as shown here.

4 **Cut one T-shirt strip in half.** Discard the other half. Now you have two strips, one twice as long as the other. The T-shirt we used yielded a 26-inch piece and a 52-inch piece.

5 **Tie a piece of string to the end of one of the sticks.** If you have a drill with a small bit, make a hole near the end of the stick and thread the string through it. If you don't own a drill, make a small notch in the stick with a file and tie the knot there. Wrap the string around the stick a few times and tie it with a knot so it doesn't come off. Tie another knot about 1 inch farther along the string as shown. Make sure you have about 2 inches or more of string beyond the last knot (you'll need it to attach the T-shirt fabric).

6 **Attach the two T-shirt strips to the string.** Start by tying the ends of the strips in a knot. Then tie the string to the strips below the knot as shown.

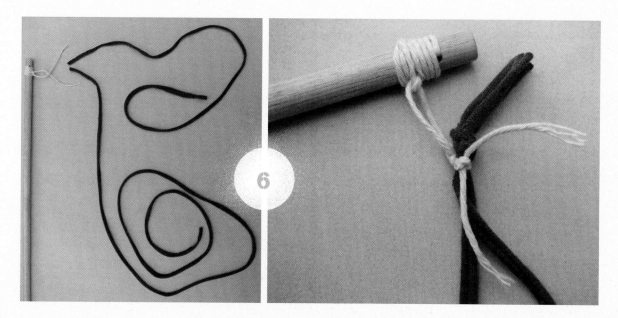

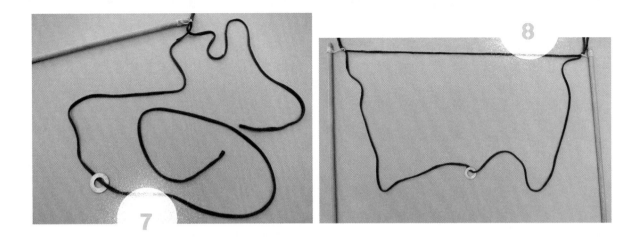

7 **Thread the longer strip through the washer.** If you don't have a large washer, two small ones will do. You can also use a metal nut.

8 **Attach the T-shirt strips to the other stick.** Repeat steps 5 and 6 with the other stick.

Your wand is done!

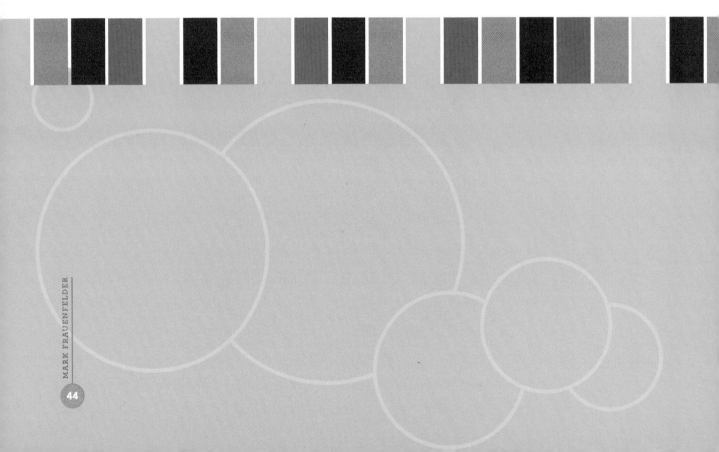

How to Use the Giant Bubble Wand

1 **Find a suitable place outdoors.** A gentle breeze is nice, but calm air will work, too. If the wind is gusty, it will be challenging to create large bubbles.

2 **Pour bubble solution into a plastic bucket or bowl until it's about 2 inches deep.** Dip the business ends of the sticks into the bubble solution and get the strips thoroughly soaked. It's okay to gently agitate the sticks in the solution to get them soaked, but don't vigorously stir up the mixture. That will create unwanted foam and cause the wick to tangle.

3 **Slowly lift the sticks from the solution and move them apart from each other.** The key is to move slowly and gently. Sudden, abrupt movements will cause the bubble film to pop before you are able to produce a bubble.

4 **Release the bubbles.** If there's a light breeze, allow it to blow against the bubble film to start a bubble. If there's not a light breeze, you can slowly walk backward to create a relative wind. Another method is to spin in a circle and create a curved bubble that envelops you. It's up to you when to close the wands together to seal off the bubble. Don't get discouraged if your first attempts are not successful. Making giant bubbles requires a bit of practice.

5 **Take photos and videos.** Giant bubbles are fun to photograph and video. With image-editing software, you can really bring out the colors in the bubbles.

CREATE A PODCAST

Broadcast your own show to a potential
audience of 2 billion people

In the 1990s, if you wanted to start a radio station you would have had to buy hundreds of thousands of dollars' worth of broadcasting equipment. You'd have to hire people to operate the equipment. You'd need a building to hold all the people and equipment. You'd need an expensive license from the Federal Communications Commission. And after all that, your radio signal would cover only a small portion of the country.

What a difference fifteen years makes! Today, you can do everything a radio station does and more for a fraction of the cost. With your computer, an Internet connection, and an inexpensive microphone, you can create a show that any of the planet's 2.4 billion Internet users can listen to. These shows are called podcasts, and there are more than one hundred thousand podcasts covering every subject you can imagine. Podcast episodes are stored as sound files on the Internet, and people subscribe to have each new episode of a podcast sent to their mobile phone or computer to listen to at their convenience. Apple's iTunes has a huge directory of podcasts that you can browse through and subscribe to for free. Visit makerdad.org for a link to Apple's directory of podcasts for kids and family.

For the last couple of years, Jane and I have been producing a podcast called *Apps for Kids* (appsforkidspodcast.com). In each episode we review one of our favorite mobile phone apps and respond to listeners' e-mail questions. It's fun to hear from listeners who enjoy the show, and we like to keep track of how many people download the podcast.

In this project, we'll show you how to produce your own podcast and share your episodes with listeners online.

COMPUTER

- **Microphone** (See Part 3: Recording the Episode for advice on what kind of microphone to use.)
- **Audio recording and editing software.** If you use a Mac, we recommend GarageBand. Otherwise, you can download the free Audacity program for PCs.

How to Make a Podcast

There are five basic parts to making a podcast:

1. Setting up your podcast
2. Planning your episode
3. Recording the episode
4. Editing the episode
5. Publishing the episode

PART 1: SETTING UP YOUR PODCAST

Before you record your first episode, it's a good idea to name the podcast, write a description, design a logo for it, and find a place to store the sound files. There are many different ways to do this, but an excellent way to get started is to use podomatic.com's free service. That's what we'll use to set up our sample podcast.

1 **Design a logo.** Use a drawing program, such as Adobe Illustrator, to create a square logo. It should be 600 pixels per side. Include the name of your podcast. Keep the design simple and bold, because it will often appear on phones and other websites as a tiny square. Save the art as a JPEG file.

2 **Set up a hosting service.** After registering for a free account on podomatic.com, click the Publish tab at the top of the page and choose Podcast, then Settings from the drop-down menu. Fill out the form with information about your podcast, such as a title, a tagline, and a description. Upload your logo. Select a category from the pull-down menu, and add a few tags (these are key words that will cause your podcast to appear in online search results). Select the language your podcast is in and then click Save.

1

Basic Info | Comments | Design | iTunes | Sidebar | Ads

Edit your title, cover art, category, and more.

Podcast URL: makerdad.podomatic.com

Title: Maker Dad

Tagline: Cool Projects for Dads and Kids

☑ Display Title and Tagline in the page masthead

Cover art: Choose a photo from your media library:
maker-dad-podcast-logo.jpg ⬦

Description: Do you and your kids want to make cool things like giant bubble wands, silk-screen T-shirts, skateboards, video cameras that attach to kites, musical instruments, and video games? This is the podcast where

Category: Kids & Family

Tags: dad diy family fun how-to maker makers project
(separated by spaces)

Language: English (United States)

Apply these changes to my...
☑ Podcast page - Settings   ☐ Duplicate Title, Tagline & Description changes across these pages
☑ Premium page - Settings
☑ Events page - Settings

Save   Saved Revert to last saved

2

Optional: Create or select theme music and sound effects for your show. You have several options for creating or buying theme songs and transition sounds (to separate one part of a show from another). You can record yourself playing a musical instrument and use that. Or you can use a cool mobile application like nodebeat.com to generate a theme song (a). The easiest way to get a theme song is to buy one for a few dollars from a site like pond5.com. For sound effects (used to transition from one part of your program to the next), you can record yourself playing a slide whistle or a Jew's harp, or making funny sounds with your mouth. You can also find a lot of fun effects at freesound.org. Avoid using music that is under copyright because you could get into legal trouble if you don't have permission.

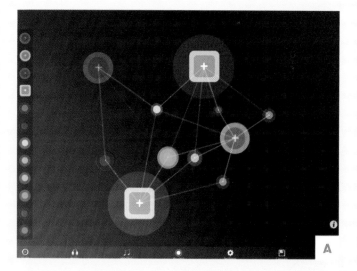

A

PART 2: PLANNING YOUR EPISODE

Podcasting is a performance, and every performance needs a script or an outline. Before you start recording the show, take a little time to plan. It will make things easier when it comes time to edit your podcast, and your audience will enjoy the show more if it has a clear structure. Here's a sample outline:

MAKER DAD PODCAST EPISODE 001

Introduction

MARK: Hello, parents and kids! Welcome to episode one of the *Maker Dad* podcast, brought to you by the *Maker Dad* book, available on amazon.com. I'm your cohost Mark Frauenfelder.

JANE: I'm your cohost Jane Frauenfelder. In this month's episode of the *Maker Dad* podcast, we're going to talk about the best ways to make giant bubbles.

(Transition Music)

Mark and Jane discuss the Giant Bubbles project in the book and give tips for getting great bubbles:

• *Bubble solution recipe*

• *Best kind of wick to use*

• *Holding and opening the wand*

• *What to do when there's no wind*

• *Where to go to see cool giant bubble videos*

(Transition Sound Effect)

MARK: If you'd like to learn how we made giant bubbles, visit makerdad.org to order a copy of my new book, *Maker Dad: Lunch Box Guitars, Antigravity Jars, and 22 Other Incredibly Cool Father–Daughter DIY Projects.*

JANE: Besides making giant bubbles, the book will show you how to make a guitar out of a lunch box, how to program your own retro arcade game, how to make soap in the shape of your thumb, how to make astronaut ice cream, how to make a robot that draws on paper, even how to make your own podcast. All these and much more in *Maker Dad*.

MARK: We will be back next month with another episode of the *Maker Dad* podcast!

(Outro Music)

PART 3: RECORDING THE EPISODE

No matter how interesting your podcast is, if the sound quality isn't good, no one is going to listen to it. That's why it's important to record your podcast in a room that has good acoustics. Recording in a room with hardwood floors creates an echo. If you have a room with a thick carpet and drapes covering the windows, chances are it will work well as a recording studio. If you have a laptop, a great option is to record your podcast inside a car with the doors closed and the windows rolled up. The interior of a car is an excellent recording studio because cars are made to be acoustically quiet.

1 **Select a microphone.** For one-person podcasts, you will need a headset with a mic. The iMicro IM320 USB Headset costs under $15 and works surprisingly well for the price. If you want to record a show with two or more people in the same room, you need a microphone that you can all talk into. The Tiki microphone by Blue Microphones (about $50) is a good choice. Plug the microphone into your computer and choose it as the audio input source in your computer's settings. (Most computers have a built-in microphone, but we don't recommend them because the sound quality is poor.)

2 **Set up your recording application.** You can use any recording application you like, but we'll show you how to use Audacity because it's free and easy to use. Download it from audacity.sourceforge.net. After you open Audacity, go to Preferences and select your microphone as the audio input.

3 **Test the sensitivity of your microphone.** Press the red record button in the top control panel of Audacity and speak into the microphone for a few seconds. Stop recording by pressing the square button, and press the green play arrow to listen. If it sounds too soft, adjust the input slider bar to the right (it's also in the top control bar—it has a small image of a microphone next to it). If the blue-colored waveform extends past the top and bottom of the audio track box that means your signal is "clipping" (as shown here) and you'll need to move the input slider bar to the left. After adjusting the sensitivity, record your voice again with the new settings and give it a listen. If it's still not right, try again until you are happy with the sound quality. Delete the test track by clicking the small X located in the upper left corner of the track frame.

2

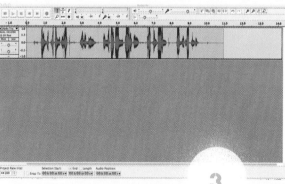

3

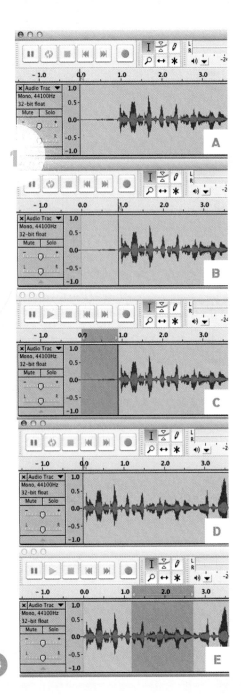

4 **Record the podcast.** Delete any test tracks by clicking the X in the upper left corner of the track frame. Click the red record button and start talking. If you make a mistake, don't stop, just start the sentence over and keep going. You can edit out the mistakes in the editing process. Once you are finished, press the square button to stop recording.

PART 4: EDITING THE EPISODE

We used Audacity to record the episode, and we'll use it to edit it, too.

1 **Delete the parts of the recording you don't want.** First, click the "skip to start" button on the control panel (the purple button with the double arrows pointing left) (a). That moves the edit cursor to the beginning of the recording. Look at the screenshot here. You'll see that the first second of the recording is silent (b). We want to remove that part of the recording. To do that, move the cursor (it looks like the letter I) to the point where you want the podcast to start, then click the mouse button. A vertical line appears at that point in the track (c). Now click Edit and select Split from the menu. The line will turn white and a bit thicker. Double click the track on the left side of the white line to highlight it and press the Delete key on your keyboard. The highlighted portion of the track will go away (d).

You can review your recording by clicking the green play button. If you find a part of the recording you want to delete, first press the brown stop button, then click and drag the unwanted portion of the track to highlight it. Press the C button on your keyboard to preview the cut. Then press the Delete key on your keyboard to delete that portion (e).

Tip: Use the magnifying glass icons with the + and – in them to zoom in and out of your recording waveform.

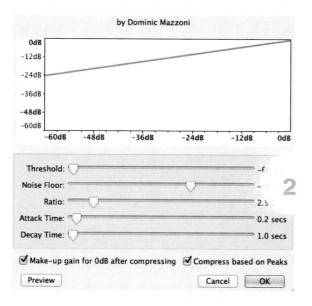

by Dominic Mazzoni

0dB
−12dB
−24dB
−36dB
−48dB
−60dB

−60dB   −48dB   −36dB   −24dB   −12dB   0dB

Threshold: _____ −f
Noise Floor: _____ −
Ratio: _____ 2.5
Attack Time: _____ 0.2 secs
Decay Time: _____ 1.0 secs

☑ Make-up gain for 0dB after compressing ☑ Compress based on Peaks

[Preview]   [Cancel] [OK]

2 **Automatically level the volume.** It's a good idea to adjust the volume of the recording (especially if you have two or more people speaking on the podcast) so that the soft parts and the loud parts aren't too extreme. This is easy to do. Click Effect and select Compressor from the menu, make sure both checkboxes, are checked and click OK.

3 **Add your recorded music file** (if you have one). Just drag the file into the Audacity window. It will probably appear as a stereo file (with two waveforms) (a). Let's convert it to a mono track to keep things simple. In the music track, click on the small black downward-pointing arrow to reveal a pop-up window (b). Then select Split Stereo to Mono. This will turn the stereo track into two mono tracks (c). Delete one of them (it doesn't matter which one) by clicking the small X in the upper left corner of the track. (If the music track waveform looks a lot smaller than the recorded voice waveform, double click the waveform then select Compressor from the Effect menu.)

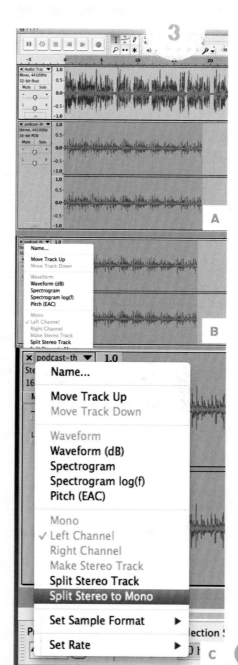

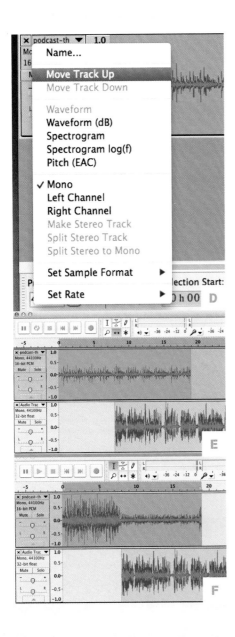

Move the music track to the top of the Audacity window by selecting Move Track Up from the track's pop-up menu (d).

We want the music to start playing before the voice recording starts, so we are going to use something called the Time Shift Tool. You can find it at the top of the Audacity window. Its icon is a short line with arrows pointing in either direction. First, click the voice track, then click the Time Shift Tool. Shift the waveform to the right. Somewhere between 5 and 10 seconds to the right is good (e).

Double click on the music waveform and select Auto Duck from the Effect menu. This will cause the music to fade when the voice recording starts to play (f).

If you have music to play at the end of the podcast, just repeat these steps.

PART 5: PUBLISHING THE EPISODE

1 **Export the podcast as an MP3 file.** From Audacity's File menu, select Export. Choose MP3 from the pull-down menu, then click Options. Under Bit Rate Mode, specify Constant. Quality should be set to 64 kbps. Under Variable Speed, select Fast, and under Channel Mode, select Stereo. Click OK and give the file a name and click Save. You will see some other dialog boxes appear, but just click OK without changing anything.

2 Upload the MP3 file to podomatic.com. Log in to your account at podomatic.com and click the New Episode button. Follow the step-by-step instructions for describing and uploading your episode, adding an episode-specific image (optional) and tags to indicate the subject of your podcast (to help potential listeners find out about the podcast). You can schedule the podcast to be published at a time and date in the future or immediately.

In either case, as soon as it is done, share the news with your friends via Facebook, Twitter, and e-mail!

SILKSCREEN T-SHIRT

An easy way to decorate your clothes and accessories

Silkscreening is a fun way to decorate T-shirts and other articles of clothing with your artwork. About ten years ago I bought a screen printing kit. It was a lot of fun, but the process of making screens is somewhat messy and time-consuming. The process involves mixing up a batch of photosensitive emulsion liquid and painting it on a fine mesh cloth stretched over a wooden frame. It was enough of a hassle that it often kept me from wanting to pull out the kit and make screens.

But recently I discovered EZScreenPrint (ezscreenprint.com), which greatly simplifies the screen printing process. This company sells stencil sheets that have been treated with the photo emulsion solution. All you need to do is clip a piece of art (that's been printed on a transparent sheet of plastic) onto the chemically treated stencil sheet and expose it to bright sunlight for 1 minute. When the sunlight hits the emulsion on the parts of the stencil that are not hidden by the black lines of the artwork, the emulsion gets hard and cannot be wiped off with water. The emulsion that is underneath the opaque artwork remains "unfixed" and is easily removed by spraying water on the stencil. That leaves you with a screen that will allow screen printing ink to pass through the lines and shapes of the artwork, allowing you to make prints on your clothes.

In this project we will show you how to decorate a T-shirt using your hand-drawn or computer-generated artwork.

THINGS YOU NEED TO MAKE A SILKSCREEN T-SHIRT

MATERIALS

- **Computer paper**
- **EZScreenPrint Basic Starter Kit, Standard.** About $40. It includes: exposure frame, 2 EZScreenPrint standard stencils, 2 exposure test pieces, plastic canvas, squeegee, bristle brush, foamie sheet, 2 transparency sheets.
- **Screen printing ink**
- **Cardboard,** stiff and noncorrugated
- **Masking tape or painter's tape**

TOOLS

- **Dark felt-tip pen**
- **Scanner or digital camera,** to upload your art to your computer
- **Computer and printer,** laser or ink jet
- **Image editing software,** such as Adobe Photoshop, Adobe Illustrator, GIMP, or Pixelmator
- **4 binder clips**
- **Scissors or craft knife and safe cutting surface**

How to Make a Silkscreen T-Shirt

1   Draw a picture on a sheet of white 8.5 in. × 11 in. paper. It's best to use a dark felt-tip pen. Alternatively, you can use an application like Adobe Photoshop or Illustrator to draw a picture on your computer. We decided to use this drawing that one of my daughters drew (we don't remember who drew it) when she was three or four years old.

2   Convert your drawing to a computer image and print it on a transparency sheet. (If you made your drawing on the computer, skip this step.) If you have a scanner, scan the drawing into your computer. Otherwise, take a photo of the art with a phone or digital camera and upload it to your computer. Use an image editing application of your choice to convert the art to solid black lines and shapes. In Photoshop, under Image, select Adjustments and use the Threshold slider. Print it onto a plastic transparency sheet (make sure you insert the sheet into your printer so that the nonshiny side receives the ink or toner).

3   Prepare the stencil sheet. This step needs to be done in a dimly lit room to prevent the photosensitive emulsion on the stencil sheet from becoming exposed prematurely. Also, wait until the sun is shining before you start this step, because you will need to expose the stencil to bright sunlight in step 7. Lay your printed transparency onto the plastic exposure frame. Peel the plastic protective backing from the stencil and discard the backing.

4   Lay the stencil on the transparency. The shiny side of the stencil should face down. Now you have a sandwich of the plastic exposure frame on the bottom, your printed transparency with your artwork in the middle, and the stencil on the top.

5   Lay the black foamie sheet on top of the stack. Now you have four layers. (We used an older version of the EZScreenPrint kit, which came with a black felt board instead of a black foamie sheet, but the process is the same.)

6   Clip the four layers together with binder clips.

7   Expose the stencil to bright sunlight for 1 minute. With the exposure frame facing up, expose your stencil to the sun for 1 minute.

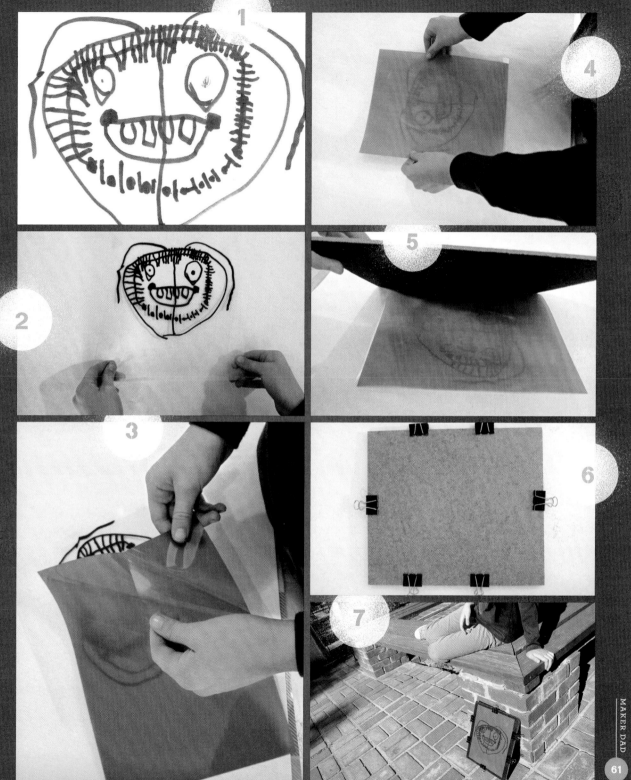

8   Soak the stencil in cool water for 15 minutes. First, remove it from the stack of other materials. You will see a faint image of your artwork in the stencil as it soaks.

9   Rinse the stencil in running water. First, place the stencil on the plastic screen, emulsion side up. Use the spray attachment on a kitchen sink faucet if you have one and spray cold water onto the stencil. Use the soft bristle brush to rub away the emulsion from the artwork. When the artwork is completely white, you can stop.

10 Dry the stencil. Keep the stencil on the plastic screen and take it outdoors to let it dry in the sun for at least half an hour. This will harden the remaining emulsion, so that the stencil can stand up to many screen prints.

11 **Make a stencil frame.** Use scissors and a stiff piece of noncorrugated cardboard to make a frame for your stencil. Make the frame's opening slightly smaller than the stencil. Make sure that the frame does not cover up any of the artwork. Use masking tape or painter's tape to attach the stencil to the frame.

Note: EZScreenPrint sells plastic frames you can use if you don't want to use a cardboard frame.

12 **Prepare your shirt for screen printing.** Start by putting a piece of cardboard underneath the first layer of fabric so the ink does not bleed through to the second layer of the garment. Then place the framed stencil on the garment.

13 **Pour about a tablespoon of screen printing ink on the framed stencil.** Put it at the top, right above the artwork.

14 **Squeegee the ink across the template.** Hold the T-shirt and template down with one hand, and with the other hand squeegee at an angle as shown and run it down the framed stencil. Once you've completely covered the artwork, carefully lift the screen partway up without disturbing its orientation so you can see whether the ink is coming through. If the screen print looks faint, lower the framed stencil onto the shirt and re-run the squeegee over the art.

15 **Allow the shirt to dry for a few days before wearing it.** This will allow the ink to completely harden so that it can stand up to washing and drying.

When it comes to screen printing, you aren't limited to clothing! You can also use screen printing to make greeting cards and posters. With the right kind of screen printing ink, you can apply art to plastic, metal, and wood in addition to paper and cloth. Once you get the hang of screen printing, try making multicolor screen prints by creating multiple templates (one for each color).

ICE CREAM SANDWICH NECKLACE

Jewelry that looks good enough to eat

Polymer clay looks and feels a lot like ordinary modeling clay. You can mold it to your heart's content without having to worry that it will dry out. It comes in a variety of brilliant colors, including sparkly metallic hues. But here's the thing that makes polymer clay so cool: once you've made something you'd like to keep, you put it in the oven at 275 degrees for about 20 minutes and it will harden into a permanent plastic object. In this project, you'll learn how to make a necklace with pieces that look like little ice cream sandwiches. After you make it, you'll be ready to make rings, charms, pins, bracelets, and other things out of polymer clay.

MATERIALS

- **Polymer clay.** The most popular brands of oven-bake clay are Sculpey and FIMO. The easiest to find, in my experience, is Sculpey, which makes several kinds of polymer clay. We recommend Sculpey III. You can buy a thirty-color sampler of polymer clay and create custom colors, which is what we will do in this project to get the right look for the cookie and Neapolitan ice cream.

- **Wax paper,** to prevent the clay from sticking

- **Parchment paper**

- **Jewelry findings.** These are the little bits of hardware that you use to connect pieces of jewelry together. Get a dozen or so jump rings, which are little wire circles that you can bend open and closed with pliers. Eye screws are little screws with a loop at one end. They are great for adding loops to your polymer clay pieces. Ball chain happens to be our favorite necklace material, but you can use linked chains, leather, or string. Make sure that whatever you use will not break easily if it gets caught on something while you are wearing it. Most craft stores sell jewelry findings.

TOOLS

- **Baby wipes**

- **Deck of cards,** to help you make sheets of clay with uniform thickness

- **Short piece of plastic sprinkler pipe.** A good roller for flattening the clay. You can also use a highlighter as a roller instead.

- **Bowl,** to cover the clay from dust

- **Mini cookie cutters,** to cut the clay into shapes

- **Straightened paper clip,** for poking holes in the clay

- **Craft knife,** to cut the clay

- **Cutting board, self-healing cutting pad, or pane of glass**

- **Cookie sheet**

- **2 needle-nose pliers,** to open and close the jump rings

How to Make an Ice Cream Sandwich Necklace

1 **Mix your clay colors.** These ice cream sandwiches use four colors of clay: dark brown, light brown, cream, and pink. To make these colors you will need to mix several clays in your sampler. Use dark brown to make the cookie, dark brown and white to make the chocolate ice cream, white with a bit of yellow to make the vanilla ice cream, and white with a pinch of red for the strawberry ice cream. Knead the clay compounds until the colors are completely mixed. The balls of clay should be a bit smaller than a Ping-Pong ball.

Note: After mixing a color, clean your hands and the work surface thoroughly to prevent lighter colors from getting stained by the darker colors. We keep a supply of baby wipes on hand and use them frequently.

2 **Roll the cookie clay.** Set some wax paper on the work surface. Make two stacks of ten playing cards and lay them on either side of the blob of cookie clay. Use your roller to flatten the clay into a uniformly thick sheet that's larger than the diameter of the cookie cutters you have and matches the thickness of the ten playing cards.

Note: If you see a bubble in your flattened clay that means there's air trapped under the surface. You don't want bubbles because they will cause the clay to crack when you heat it in the oven. If your clay sheet has a bubble, lift it up, knead it well, and reflatten it with the roller.

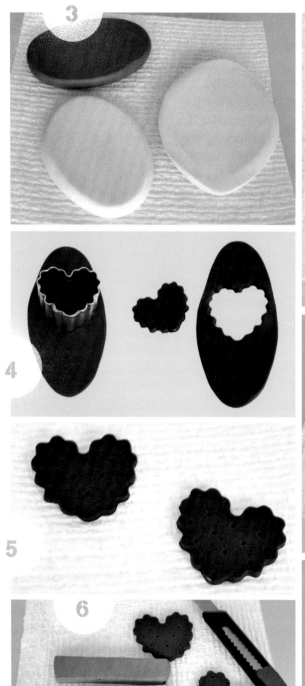

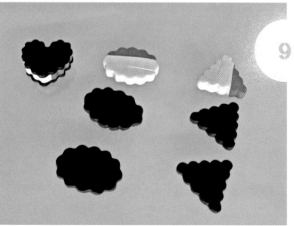

3   Roll the ice cream clay. Wipe down the roller with a baby wipe to prevent the new colors from getting stained by residual clay stuck on the roller. Clean your hands, too. Repeat step 2 for the three colors of ice cream clay, except use twenty-five cards on each side instead of just ten, because the ice cream should be thicker than the cookie. Set the sheets of clay on wax paper and cover them with a bowl to prevent dust from sticking to their surfaces.

4   Cut the cookie clay. Press the cookie cutter into the sheet of cookie clay. Carefully push out the piece that's inside the cutter and set it on the wax paper. If the sheet isn't big enough to cut out two cookies, just roll up the remaining clay into a ball and re-roll it into a sheet and cut out the other cookie.

5   Poke holes in the cookies. Use a straightened paper clip to poke holes in the cookie. You don't need to go all the way through the clay—just make a dent in the surface. If you mess up the pattern, wad your clay up into a ball and start over from step 2.

Note: If you want a simple pendant necklace with a single ice cream flavor, you can skip the next two steps.

6   Cut the ice cream clay. This part is a bit tricky. You need to cut strips from the three flavors of ice cream clay. The three strips should be of equal width, and their combined widths should be the same as the width of the cookie. Place the clay sheets on wax paper and place the wax paper on a surface that's safe to cut on (such as a cutting board, self-healing cutting pad, or pane of glass). Carefully cut the strips with a craft knife.

7   Stick the ice cream clay strips together. Place the three ice cream strips together, side by side, on a piece of wax paper. Place two stacks of twenty-two playing cards on either side. With the roller (did you remember to clean it with a fresh baby wipe?), go over the strips. The downward pressure of the roller will help the strips stick together.

8   Cut the ice cream clay. Make sure the cookie cutter is clean. Place the ice cream clay on wax paper and cut out the shape. Carefully push it out of the cookie cutter. You now have all the pieces made for one ice cream sandwich. Place them together and gently apply even pressure to make the cookies stick to the ice cream center.

9   Make more sandwiches. Repeat steps 2 through 8 to make more ice cream sandwiches. We made three for our necklace, but you can make more if you want a really chunky necklace. You can also try different colors of ice cream and cookies if you want to increase the variety of treats.

10 **Bake the clay.** Set your oven (or toaster oven if you have one) to 275 degrees Fahrenheit. Once it reaches temperature, place the ice cream sandwiches on a cookie sheet lined with parchment paper and put it on a rack in the oven. (The temperature is low enough to prevent the paper from burning, but make sure the paper doesn't touch the heating element). Bake for 30 minutes. Remove the cookie sheet with the sandwiches on it (careful, they're hot) and let them cool to room temperature. They are now hard and ready for the next step.

11 **Add eye screws and jump rings.** Twist an eye screw into the ice cream sandwich. Don't overtighten it. Next, use two pairs of pliers to open a jump ring. Don't open the ring by pulling apart the gap. Instead, open it by twisting your wrists in opposite directions (like wringing out a washcloth) so the ends slide past each other. Put the jump ring through the eye screw and close it up with the pliers. Repeat this step for each ice cream sandwich.

12 **String clay pieces on the chain.** Now, run the chain through the jump rings. If you want to keep the pieces from clustering together at the bottom of the chain, squeeze the jump rings tight around the ball chain. If you are using a linked chain, you can open the jump rings and insert them through the chain links. If you are using string, you can tie knots to lock the pieces in place.

The sky is the limit when it comes to polymer clay. You can make anything you want out of it: turn it into jewelry (e.g., a charm bracelet made out of fruits) or use it for other purposes (e.g., doll house food).

Above: The eyes for this skull were made with a Phillips-head screwdriver.

Left: Red clay and black paint give this skull's eyes a spooky stare.

Next page: A–D: Silicone molding putty is a fun and easy way to make casts of trinkets you want to copy. Make the silicone molding putty by mixing the two parts, then press your original piece into it and let it cure for a couple of hours. Remove your original piece and press a blob of polymer clay into the mold. Then put the silicone mold and clay into the toaster oven (275 degrees Fahrenheit) for 15–30 minutes.

Next page: E–F: We used different objects with interesting patterns on them to make these funny faces.

POLYMER CLAY NECKLACE GALLERY

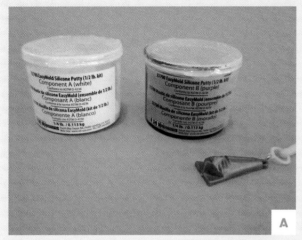

A

B

C

D

E

F

PAPER BOWL
SPEAKER

Music from a magnet, a wire, and some paper

Do you know how a speaker works? Electrical signals from an MP3 player or stereo system travel through wires. The signal looks like this:

The strength of the electrical signal matches the changes in volume and frequency of the sound signal. When this electrical signal reaches the speaker, it hits a coil of wire that surrounds a magnet. The coil is attached to a speaker cone made of paper. The permanent magnet is attached to the back of the speaker. When the electrical signal coming from the wire enters the coil, the coil turns into an electromagnet. The permanent magnet and the coil of wire interact with each other. Sometimes the two magnets oppose each other, causing the speaker cone to be pushed away from the magnet. Other times the two magnets attract each other, causing the speaker cone to move toward the permanent magnet. This back and forth motion happens very fast, faster than the eye can see. The rapid back-and-forth motion of the speaker cone creates sound waves, which hit your eardrum, creating the sound of whatever the MP3 player is playing.

It's very easy to make your own speaker. In this project, we'll show you how to make a speaker you can attach to your wall with parts costing less than a couple of dollars. This project was inspired by inventor José Pino's homemade speaker projects. Check out all of his fun projects at josepino.com.

THINGS YOU NEED TO MAKE A PAPER BOWL SPEAKER

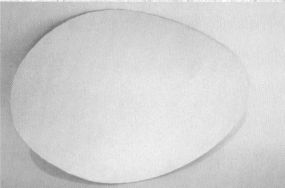

MATERIALS

- **Spray paint, or paint and brushes**
- **Rigid paper or Styrofoam bowl**
- **Sheet of cardboard.** It should be larger than the diameter of the bowl you are using.
- **Sheet of printer paper**
- **Neodymium or other strong magnets,** ½-inch diameter is good. If they are thin magnets, use 2 or 3 to make a stack between ½ to ¾ inch tall.
- **Clear tape**
- **Spool of magnet wire,** such as RadioShack model #278-1345
- **Pair of old earbuds you are willing to sacrifice**
- **Business card**

TOOLS

- **Scissors or paper cutter**
- **Hot glue gun and hot glue sticks**
- **Wire cutters**
- **Needle-nose pliers**
- **Sandpaper,** various grits
- **Wire strippers**
- **30-watt pen-type soldering iron and rosin-core solder**
- **Solder sucker or a spool of desoldering wick,** so you can remove solder easily

How to Make a Paper Bowl Speaker

1. **Paint or decorate the paper bowl and cardboard.** The cardboard can be cut with scissors to any shape you like. You don't need to paint the outside bottom, as it will be hidden from view.

2. **Cut two strips from the sheet of printer paper.** Make them 11 inches long and ¾ inch wide. Wind the first strip tightly around the magnet (or stack of magnets if you are using more than one) and fasten the end with a bit of tape to keep it from unraveling. Then take the second strip and wind it around the first strip, taping down the loose end.

3. **Attach the coiled paper strips to the bowl.** Remove the magnet from the coiled paper. Turn the bowl upside down and hot glue the coil as close to the middle as possible. When the hot glue hardens, drop the magnet back in. Tape one end of the magnet wire to the outside of the paper coil with about 12 inches dangling from the end.

4

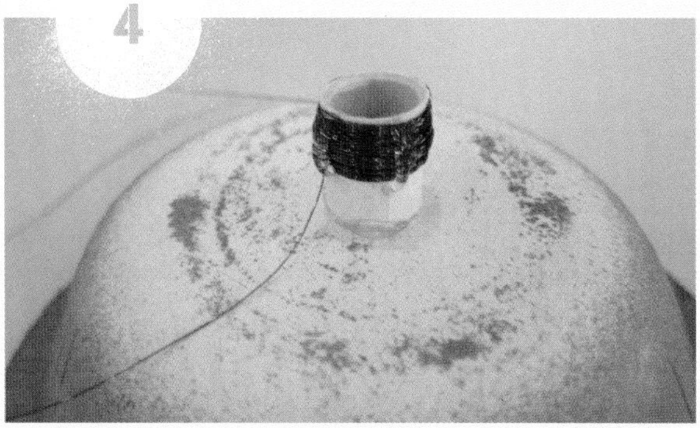

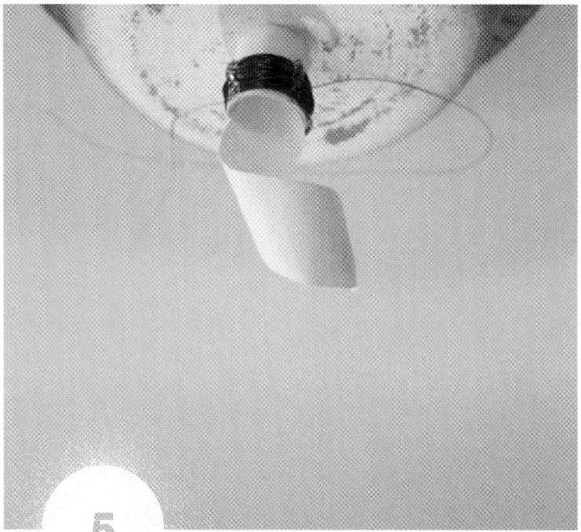

5

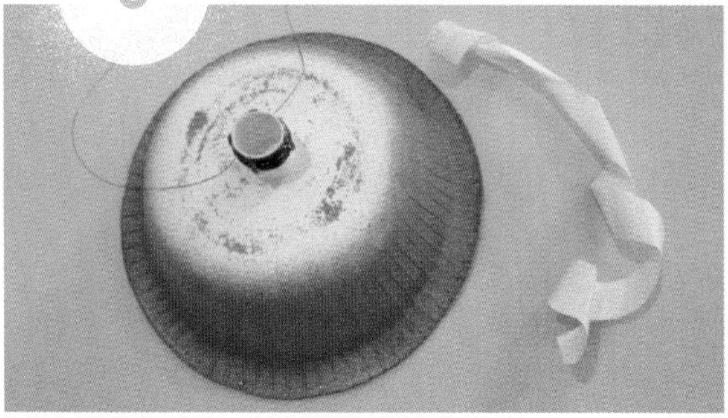

6

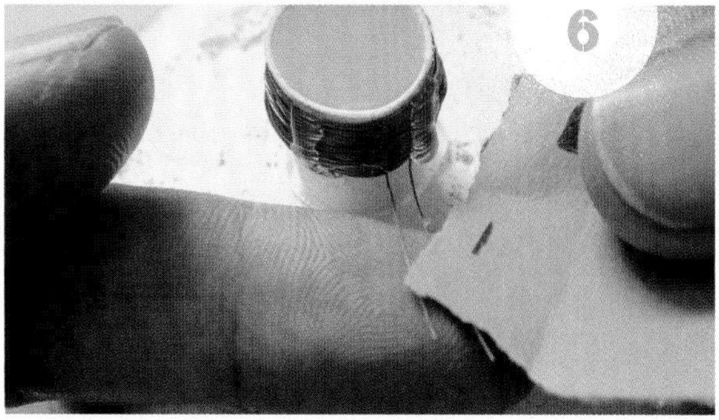

7

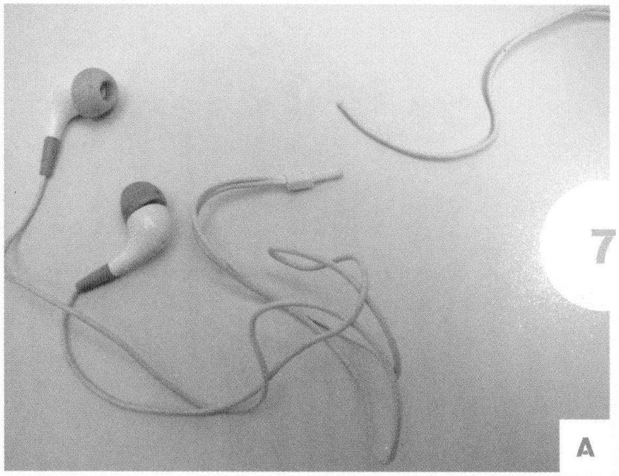

A

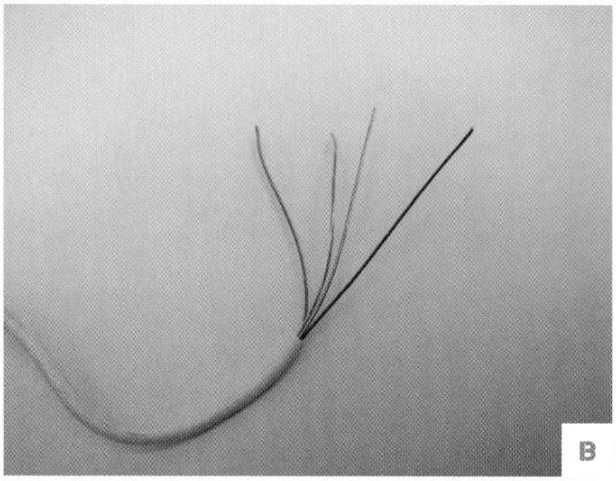

B

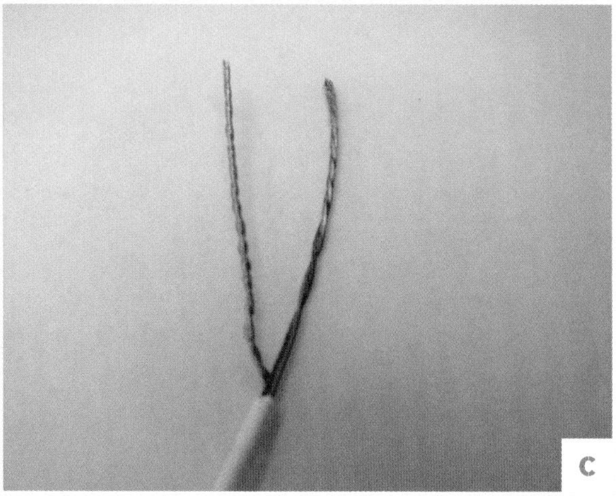

C

4 **Wind the wire around the paper coil.** Wind the wire around the paper coil about one hundred times. Add a few lines of hot glue along the coil to prevent the wires from unraveling. Clip the spool end of the wire with wire cutters to leave 12 inches dangling from the coil.

5 **Remove the magnet and the inner coil of paper.** Carefully pull out the inner coil of paper. You may want to use a pair of needle-nose pliers to pinch the end. Pull it out and discard it.

6 **Strip the insulation from the magnet wire.** Use the sandpaper to lightly rub the wire, removing the plastic varnish from the wire. Don't rub too hard or you will scrape away the copper wire. You can tell that you've removed the varnish when the wire is the color of a new penny.

7 **Prepare the earbud wires.** Clip the earbud cable right below the point where the cable splits in two (a). Strip a couple of inches of the cable's insulation with wire strippers. You'll find four wires inside. Two are copper colored, one is red, and one is green (b). The copper-colored ones probably don't have insulation on them, but to be safe, rub the last ½ inch with the sandpaper, then twist them together. Remove ½ inch of the red and green insulation from the other two wires and twist them together (c).

8 **Solder the earbud wires to the coil wires.** Solder one twisted pair of earbud wires to one of the coil's wires. Solder the other pair of earbud wires to the other coil wire. Attach the solder junctions to the paper bowl with a generous amount of hot glue. This will prevent the wires from breaking if the cable gets pulled.

9 **Attach the "springs."** Cut a business card into four ½-inch-wide strips. Fold each of them into a W shape and hot glue them to the bowl as shown.

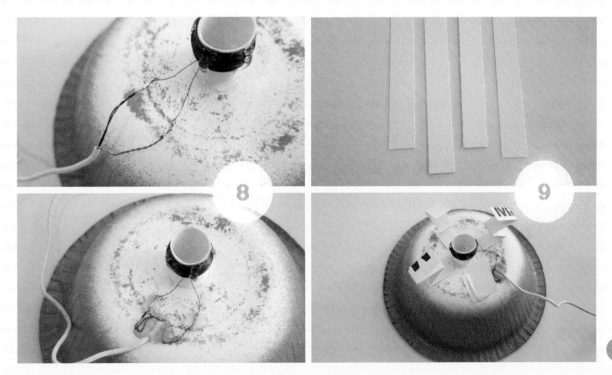

10   **Attach the magnet to the cardboard.** Use a dab of hot glue to affix it to the cardboard.

11   **Poke a hole in the cardboard for the earbud cord.** Make the hole about 1 inch away from the magnet.

12   **Glue the four "springs" to the cardboard.** Put a blob of hot glue on each of the four springs, then put the coil (attached to the bowl) over the magnet. Use a pencil to push the business card springs against the cardboard to flatten the hot glue. Push the earbud connector through the hole. Tack down the earbud cable on the back of the cardboard with a blob of hot glue.

13   **Plug the earbud connector into an MP3 player.** Play some music. The sound will be fairly soft, since the signal coming from an MP3's earbud jack isn't very strong. If you plug it into an amplified sound source, it will be much louder. Another option is to add an amplifier to the speaker. Visit makerdad.org for a link to a simple amplifier you can make yourself and add to the speaker.

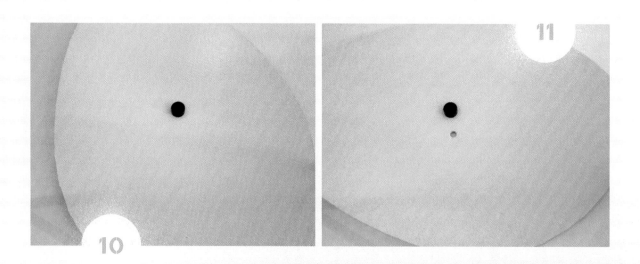

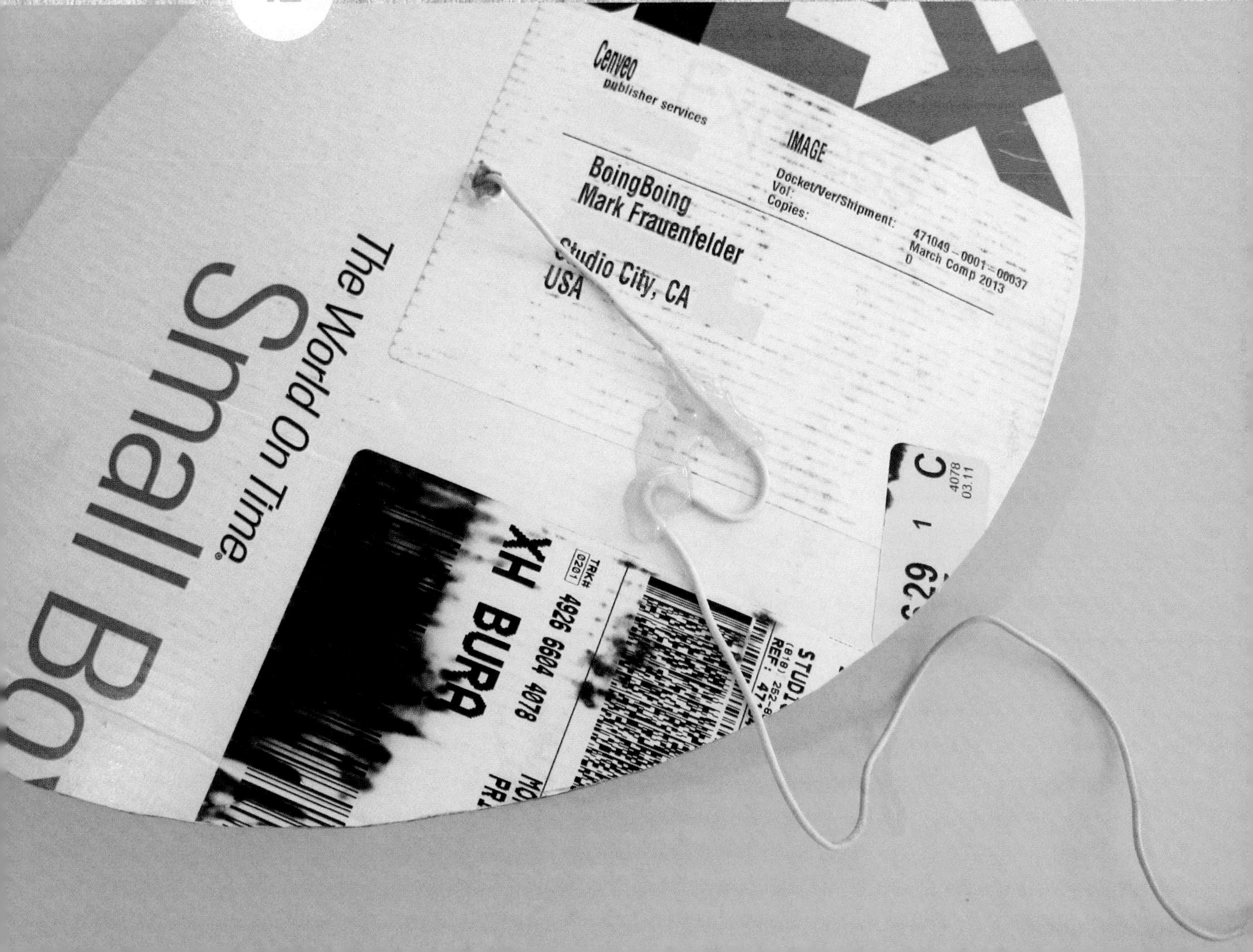

Cenveo
publisher services

IMAGE

BoingBoing
Mark Frauenfelder

Studio City, CA
USA

Docket/Ver/Shipment: 471049 - 0001 = 00037
Vol: March Comp 2013
Copies: D

C
4078
03.11

Small Bo

The World On Time.

XH
BURA

4926 6604 4078

TRK#
D291

STUDI
(818)
REF: 252-8

629 1

MO
PR

PEG TRICK

Only you know how to remove the wooden peg from the hole

The peg trick has been around for at least twenty years. It consists of a round peg and a block with a hole in it. Place the peg in the hole and challenge your friends to remove the peg without touching the block it's in. They will try to pinch the end of the peg, but it's angled so their fingers slip off. When they finally give up, you can show them how easy it is to remove the peg—blow sharply on the peg and it will pop right out of the hole! The trick exploits a principle of fluid physics known as Bernoulli's principle: the pressure exerted by a fluid (in this case, air) is inversely proportional to the velocity of the fluid. So when you blow a burst of air across the top of the peg, the pressure on the top of the peg is reduced. The (nonmoving) air pressure on the bottom of the peg is great enough to lift the peg out of the hole!

THINGS YOU NEED TO MAKE A PEG TRICK

MATERIALS

- **1 block of wood,** 1½ in. square × 1¾ in. high
- **1 dowel,** 1 in. diameter × 1½ in. high
- **Paintbrushes and acrylic paints**
- **Polyurethane spray**

TOOLS

- **Band saw or handsaw with miter box**
- **Sharpie pen**
- **Metal or plastic ruler**
- **Wood-boring drill bit,** 1-inch diameter
- **Drill press or hand drill**
- **Sandpaper,** various grits
- **Rotary tool with sanding drum**

How to Make the Peg Trick

1 **Cut the block and dowel to length.** A band saw will make quick work of this, but you can also use an inexpensive handsaw and miter box.

2 **Drill a hole in the block.** Use a Sharpie pen and ruler to mark the drill bit 1⅛ inches up from the flat part of the bit (a). If you are using a drill press, insert the bit, then place the block alongside the drill bit and adjust the drill press's stop so it won't drill deeper than 1⅛ inches. If you're using a hand drill, wrap the bit with colored tape at the Sharpie pen mark (b). Center the drill bit on the block and make the hole (c).

Note: A 1-inch-diameter dowel is usually a bit less than 1 inch. It should fit loosely in the hole. If it doesn't, use sandpaper to make the hole a little bigger.

3 **Round off one end of the peg.** Use a rotary tool with a sanding drum to make a lipstick-shaped cone on one end of the peg. If you don't have a rotary tool, you can use sandpaper and patience. Test out your work by dropping the peg in the hole. If you can't pull it out by pinching it with your fingers, you are ready to move on to the next step. If you are able to pull it out with your fingers, keep sanding!

4 **Paint and varnish the peg and block.** Let both dry thoroughly before inserting the peg in the hole.

Have fun challenging your friends!

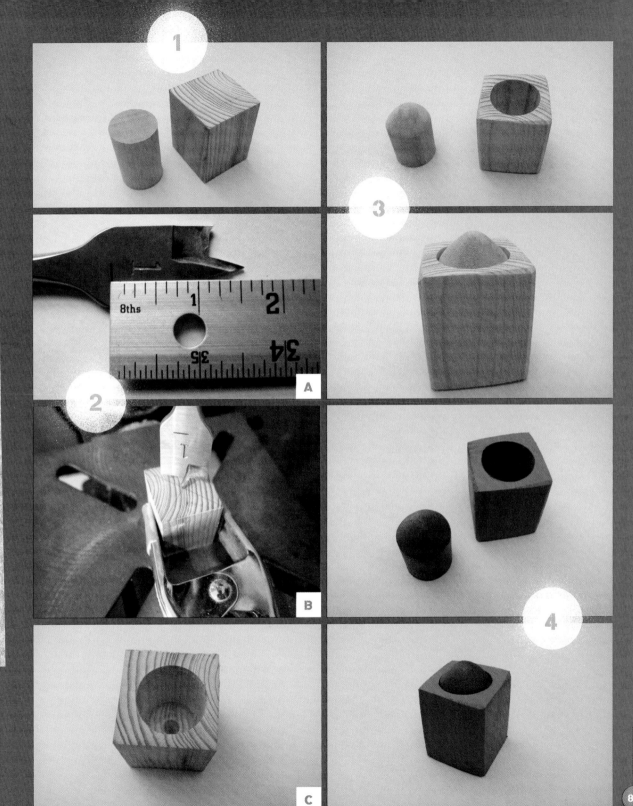

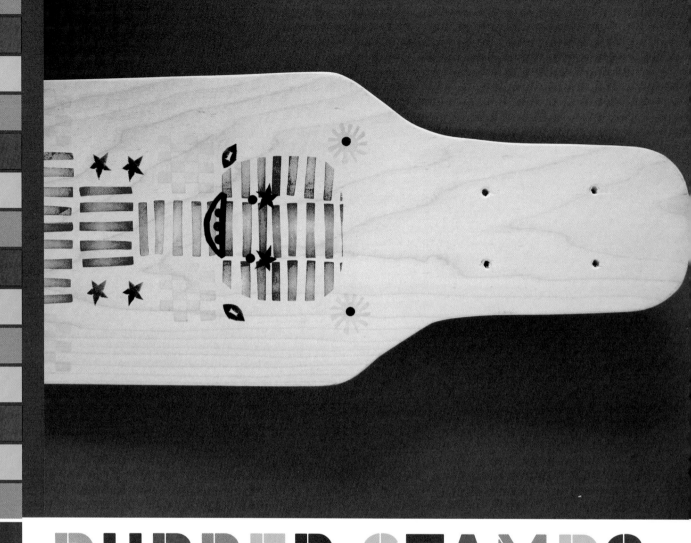

RUBBER STAMPS

Decorate paper, books, gift wrapping, and more with your own designs

Making stamps is a popular crafting activity. Most people make them by carving potatoes or erasers. But there's a better material for DIY stamps: craft foam. These thick sheets of foam have an adhesive backing that makes it easy to stick them onto blocks of wood. You can make great designs for greeting cards, stationery, and even skateboards.

THINGS YOU NEED TO MAKE RUBBER STAMPS

MATERIALS

- **Blocks of wood.** Cut them to any size you wish, keeping in mind the size of the ink pads you will use.
- **Peel-and-stick craft foam sheets.** It doesn't matter what color they are.
- **Stamp pads, various colors.** If young children are involved, consider getting pads with washable ink.
- **Something to stamp,** such as paper or unfinished wood

TOOLS

- **Saw and miter box**
- **Sandpaper,** various grits
- **Scissors or craft knife and cutting pad**

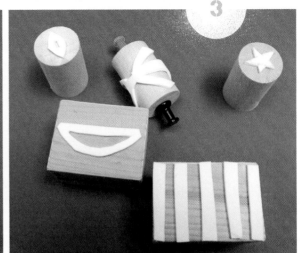

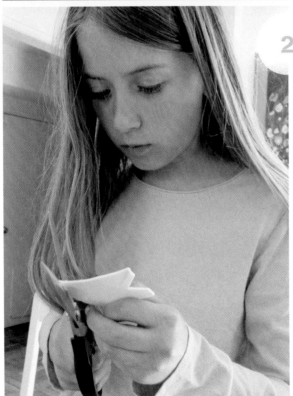

How to Make Rubber Stamps

1 **Cut the blocks of wood.** Use a miter box to keep the ends square. Sandpaper the corners and edges so the blocks are comfortable to handle.

2 **Cut the craft foam.** Use scissors or a craft knife and a cutting pad to cut the shapes you want to stamp.

We tried drawing patterns on the foam sheets and then cutting them out, but it didn't work out very well. Instead, it's better to simply cut the foam and hope for the best. If you don't like the result, just start over with a new piece of craft foam.

Note: If you are cutting out numerals or letters of the alphabet, remember to make them as mirror images.

3 **Stick the craft foam to the blocks.** Peel off the adhesive backing of the craft foam and stick the foam to the block of wood.

4 **Start stamping!** The first time you use the stamps, press them on the stamp pad and make stamps on a piece of scrap paper. Do this a few times to prime the stamp. After that, use the stamps on paper, wood, leather, and other dry, porous surfaces. Try making a roller stamp, as shown here. You can even rubber stamp on 100 percent cotton fabric by using special fabric ink.

THE FRIENDSTRUMENT

An electronic musical instrument that you
play by tapping your friend

My daughters love to show the Friendstrument to their friends, and it never fails to elicit squeals of delight when they play with it. The Friendstrument looks like a colorful keepsake box with one difference: on the lid sit two pennies. One girl touches a penny with her finger, and her friend touches the other penny. With their free hands, the girls tap each other on the arms and face. With each tap, the box emits a tone. You can vary the pitch with the amount of pressure you apply with your finger. The reason we call it the Friendstrument is because it turns friends into a musical instrument!

This is one of the more challenging projects in the book because it involves electronics and soldering. If you've never made an electronic circuit before, don't fear! The Friendstrument has a simple circuit, and you and your daughter will enjoy making it. If you've never soldered before, this is a great opportunity to learn. (Read hacker and inventor Mitch Altman's excellent comic book guide to soldering at makerdad.org.) I know parents who have taught their five-year-olds how to solder. If you aren't ready to dive in and learn soldering, we'll show you how to complete the circuit without soldering.

MATERIALS

- **Paintbrushes and acrylic paints,** or any other medium you prefer

- **Wooden box.** We went to the local craft store and bought a few wooden boxes for a dollar each. An ideal box is between 3 and 5 inches in diameter and about 3 inches tall. You can also use a cardboard box or other container that can be drilled.

- **Comic books and magazines,** to cut images from

- **Mod Podge**

- **2 transistors:** 1 NPN transistor, such as a 2N3904, and 1 PNP transistor, such as a 2N4403. They look the same, but you need one of each kind to make the circuit. These are very cheap in bulk—on eBay I bought 100 PNPs for a penny apiece and 100 NPNs for 5 cents each—so stock up and buy a bunch because you'll probably burn one or two out by mistake and it's nice to have a few spares laying around. If you can't find the models we used, that's okay—most any general-purpose, low-power transistor should work.

- **22AWG hookup wire.** RadioShack (model #278-1224) sells a 75-foot set of three spools (black, green, and red) for $8.49.

- **Solderless prototyping breadboard.** They cost under $10 and allow you to make circuits without soldering the connections. We use a large one with numbers and letters to try things out, and often use a mini solderless breadboard (about $3) to make a semipermanent circuit.

- **Short orange wire** (you can use any color you'd like, though)

- **4 resistors:** two 1M ohm resistors, one 100K ohm resistor, and one 1K ohm resistor. I bought a jumbo box of 860 different kinds of ¼-watt resistors for $20 on Amazon. Visit makerdad.org for a guide that shows you how to determine the value of a resistor by looking at its color bands.

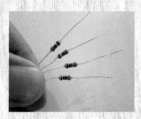

- **One 4.7-nanofarad capacitor.** I bought an assortment of 100 capacitors with different values from Amazon for $15.

- **2 AA battery holder,** similar to RadioShack model #270-408. It comes with a built-in on/off switch. They cost about $2.

- **2 AA batteries**

- **One 8 ohm mini speaker.** RadioShack model #273-092 sells for $3.99. You can also scrounge one up from a broken toy or radio or order one from Amazon or eBay.

- **2 pennies**

TOOLS

- **Scissors**
- **Glue stick**
- **Brush,** for applying the Mod Podge
- **Cardboard,** to protect your work surface
- **Wire cutters/wire strippers** (shown above in the photo of the 22AWG hookup wire)
- **30-watt pen-type soldering iron and rosin-core solder.** Available for about $10 online.

- **Solder sucker or a spool of desoldering wick,** so you can remove solder easily
- **Drill and bit**
- **Glue dots or hot glue gun and hot glue sticks**

How to Make a Friendstrument

1 **Paint the box.** You can use acrylic paints, watercolor, color markers, or any other coloring method.

2 **Find art for the box.** Collect magazines, comic books, stickers, colored paper, and other materials to put on the surfaces of the box. Use scissors to cut out images and shapes. When the paint from step 1 is dry, use a glue stick to attach your images to the box.

3 **Apply Mod Podge with a brush.** Mod Podge is a decoupage sealer and finish that will protect your decorated box and make it look shiny. One coat is usually enough.

4 **Allow the box to dry.** Find a place that's free of dust and pet fur and let the box dry for at least a few hours before handling it. While it's drying, you can move to the next steps: making the electronic circuit that produces the music.

E B C

MEET THE TRANSISTOR

Transistors are electronic components that can be used both as switches (to turn power on and off to a part of a circuit) and as amplifiers (to increase the amplitude of an electrical signal, such as a musical waveform). Most common transistors have three wires, or leads, coming out of them. One lead is an emitter (E), one is a base (B), and one is a collector (C). There are two types of transistors, NPN and PNP, and it is important to use the type called for in your circuit, or it won't work. It's easy to blow a transistor by wiring it incorrectly, but the good news is they are cheap (as little as a penny apiece). Be sure to refer to the specification sheet for the transistor you are using to see which leads are E, B, and C (they aren't always arranged as shown here). You can google the part number (e.g., 2N3904) to obtain the specification (or "spec") sheet.

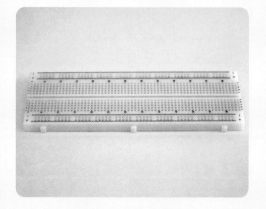

MEET THE SOLDERLESS BREADBOARD

A solderless prototyping breadboard allows you to quickly build a circuit without soldering components. Instead of using solder to join component leads, you insert the leads of components into holes in the board. A typical solderless breadboard has sixty-four numbered rows and ten columns marked A through J. Every hole in each row from A to E is connected, and every hole in each row from F to J is connected. The four outside columns, marked with red + symbols and blue - symbols, are where you'll connect the battery case wires, which are the source for the circuit's power.

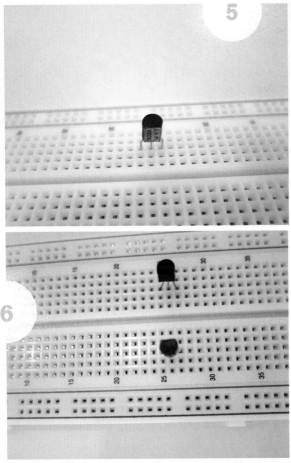

5 Insert the NPN transistor into the breadboard. E goes into hole 27C, B goes into 26C, and C goes into 25C.

Note: If you have never used a solderless breadboard, it may take a little getting used to. Use firm but gentle pressure to insert the leads into the breadboard's holes. Push them in as far as they will go. They should slide in and then stop. Don't ever force a wire or component lead into a hole—you could damage the component by breaking a lead. With practice, you will soon get comfortable using the breadboard.

6 Insert the PNP transistor. Place it on the opposite side of the breadboard from the NPN transistor, like a mirror image. E goes into hole 25H, B goes into 26H, and C goes into 27H.

7 Insert a wire between hole A27 and into any hole in the negative rail of the breadboard. Here, we used a short orange wire (you can use any color you'd like, though). The negative (-) rail is usually marked blue. This is also known as a "ground."

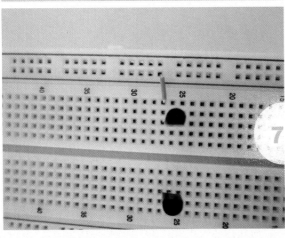

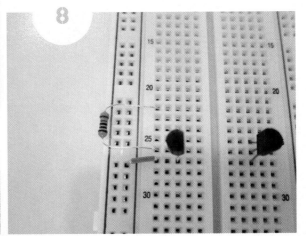

8 Insert the 100k ohm resistor into holes A22 and A26. We bent the resistor down to make it easier to see the wires. The thing to keep in mind while you build your circuit is to avoid allowing any leads to touch each other, which could cause a short circuit and possibly ruin components.

9 Insert a 1M ohm resistor into hole B26. Don't insert the other end of the resistor into the breadboard. Just let it stick out for now. This is the end that you will solder to a penny later on.

10 Insert the 1K ohm resistor into holes D25 and G26. Note that this resistor spans the middle channel dividing the two sides of the breadboard. That's just what we want.

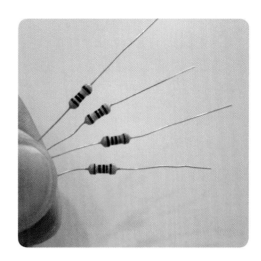

MEET THE RESISTOR

The resistor is the most common electronic component. Almost every circuit has at least one resistor. The Friendstrument uses four resistors. Their purpose is to resist the flow of electricity through the circuit. They are like kinks in a hose. The higher the value of a resistor, the more of a kink they put in the flow. They are often used to protect other components in a circuit by limiting the amount of current in the circuit. Unlike a transistor, resistors don't have polarity, so you don't have to worry about which end is which. Resistors are measured in ohms, and the symbol for ohm looks like this: W.

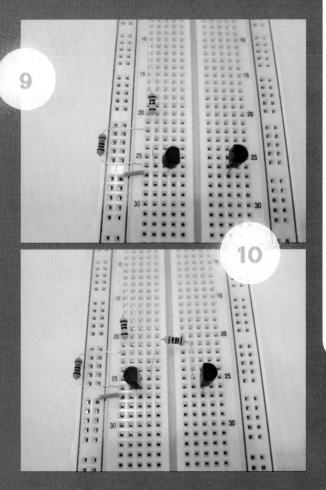

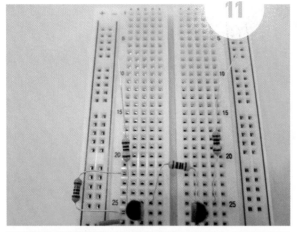

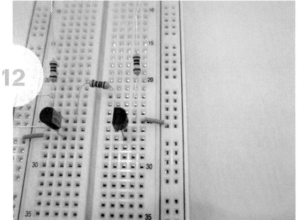

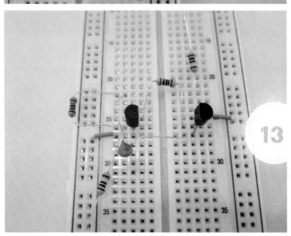

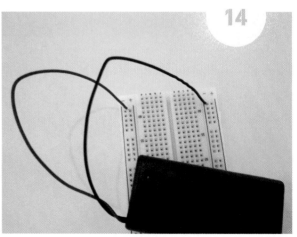

11 Insert the other 1M ohm resistor into hole I25. Don't insert the other end of the resistor into the breadboard. This is the end that will connect to the other penny.

12 Insert a wire between J25 and into any hole in the positive rail of the breadboard. The positive (+) rail is usually marked red.

13 Insert the capacitor into holes B22 and G27. This is a bit of a tight fit, so make sure that none of the leads of any components are accidentally touching each other.

14 Insert the battery holder leads. Put batteries into the holder and make sure the switch on the holder is turned off. Then insert the red wire of the battery holder into a hole in the positive rail and the black wire into a hole in the negative rail.

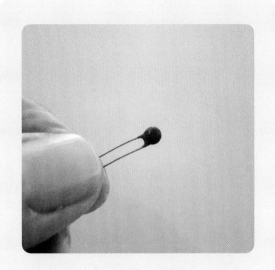

MEET THE CAPACITOR

A capacitor is kind of like a battery: it stores electrons. Unlike a battery, however, a capacitor can discharge the stored electrons very quickly. The ceramic capacitor we are using here doesn't have polarity, so you don't have to worry about which end is which. But electrolytic capacitors do have polarity and they will fail (sometimes with a bang!) if you use them backward. Also, large capacitors can deliver a dangerous electric shock if you touch both leads. The capacitor here is too small to cause any damage to you.

15 **Insert the speaker wires.** Insert one wire from the speaker into a hole in the negative rail and the other wire into J27.

16 **Test the circuit.** Make sure none of the component leads are touching other leads. Next, turn the battery holder switch to on, and hold the free wire end of one 1M ohm resistor with the finger and thumb of one hand and the other 1M ohm resistor with your other finger and thumb. The speaker should squeak. If it doesn't, check your work: Are you using fresh batteries? Did you put the transistors in correctly? Did you put any components into a wrong hole? Don't give up—you'll eventually figure out the problem!

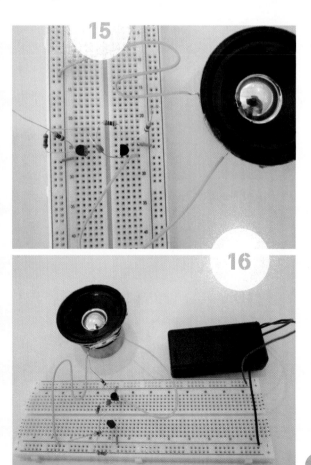

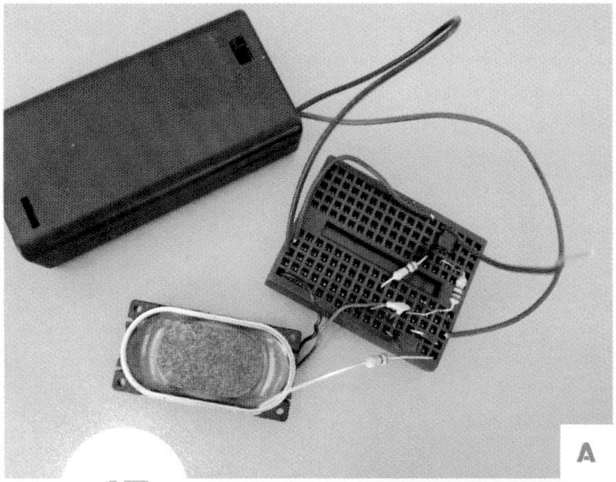

A

18

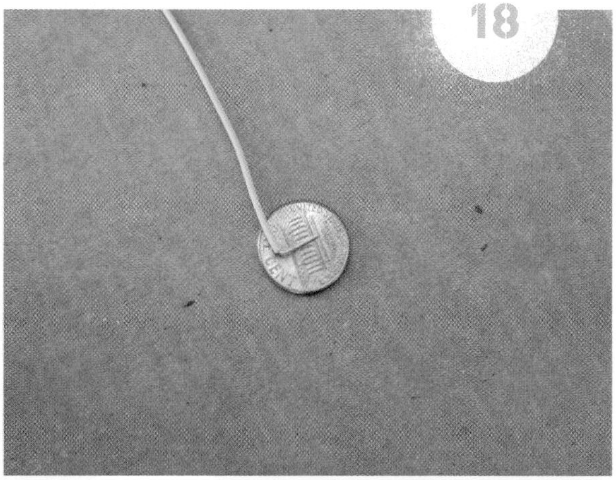

17

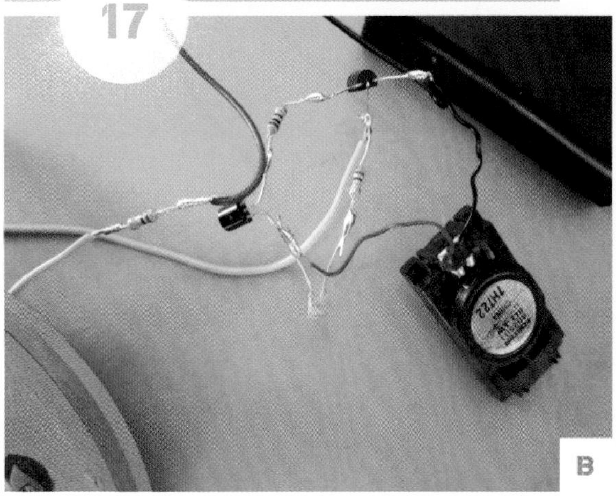

B

19

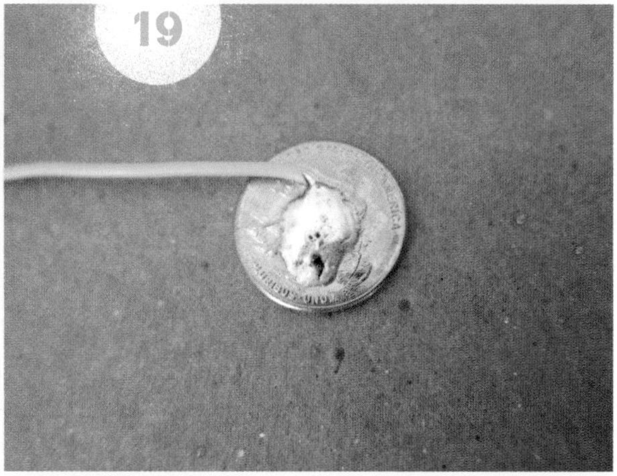

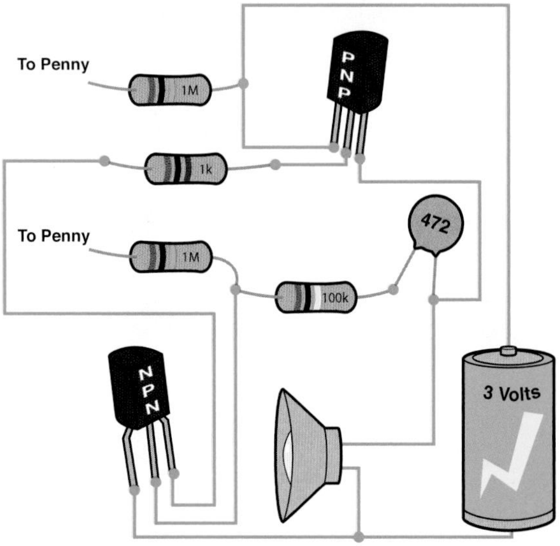
To Penny
1M
PNP
1k
To Penny
1M
472
100k
NPN
3 Volts

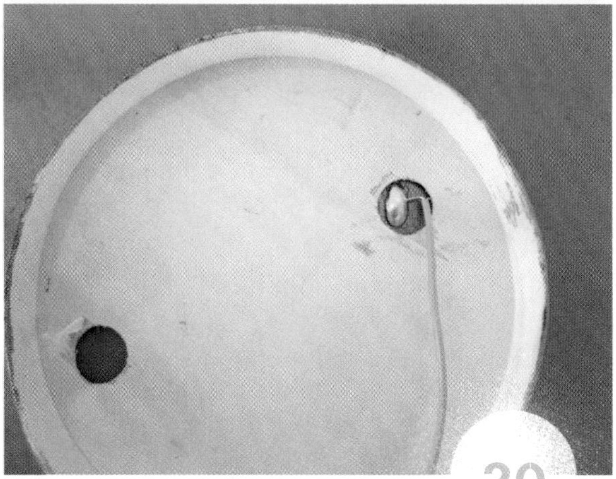

20

17 **Make a permanent circuit.** Now that you have verified that your circuit works, it's time to miniaturize it so that it fits into your box. You have at least three different options for making a permanent circuit. You can insert the components into a smaller breadboard. You can solder the components together directly. Or you can use a piece of perforated board (known as perf board) to mount the components prior to soldering them. We made circuits using the first two options. Let's look at the mini breadboard method first.

(a) **Using a mini breadboard circuit.** This is the quickest and easiest way to make a permanent circuit. The advantage is that you don't have to solder anything, and if you make a mistake you can just pull the components out and start over. The disadvantage is that a breadboard circuit is not as robust as a soldered circuit, and the components might fall out of the breadboard if they are jostled. Most mini breadboards have a peel-off adhesive back so you can stick it to the inside of your box. Note that there are no positive or negative rails. No problem. Just pick one row for positive and another row for negative.

(b) **Using a soldered circuit.** If you've never soldered before, read Mitch Altman's soldering how-to comic book (see makerdad.org) and practice soldering some pieces of wire. If you know how to solder already, go ahead and solder the leads together, making sure the leads are not so long that they will accidentally touch each other and cause a short circuit. Use the schematic shown here as your guide.

18 **Prepare the pennies.** (If you don't want to solder, buy a jar of Wire Glue [wireglue.us] and use it in place of solder.) Start with a couple of clean pennies. Place the pennies on a thick piece of cardboard. Cut two pieces of wire and strip off about ½ inch of insulation from each end.

19 **Solder the pennies.** Heat a penny with the soldering iron. Then hold the solder right next to the tip of the soldering iron. It might take a minute or two, but eventually the solder will begin to melt on the penny. Wait until a nice puddle forms as shown and then insert the end of a wire into the puddle. Remove the soldering iron and hold the wire still for at least 30 seconds to allow the solder to cool. Wait a couple of minutes to let the penny cool down before you touch it. Now, test your solder connection. Don't jerk it but pull it with firm and steady pressure. If it breaks, try again! Repeat with the other penny.

20 **Drill holes through the box for the penny wires.** Before you solder (or attach, if you are using a breadboard) the free ends of the penny wires to the rest of the circuit, drill two holes in the box you decorated. The holes should be large enough to accommodate the solder bump so that the pennies lay flat on the box. You can use glue dots or hot glue to secure the pennies to the lid.

21 Drill a hole in the bottom of the box for the battery pack on/off switch. Determine where to drill a hole in the bottom of the box so that you can access the battery pack's on/off switch. Then use glue dots or hot glue to attach the battery pack to the inside of the box.

22 Finishing up. Solder or attach the free ends of the penny wires to the free ends of the resistors and put the lid on the box.

Now it's time to try it out!

How to Play the Friendstrument

The most fun way to play the Friendstrument is with two people. First, turn it on. One person puts a finger on one penny and another person puts a finger on the other penny. Then with your free hands, touch each other on the arm, nose, ear, or any other exposed body part. The speaker will emit a tone. You can change the tone by pressing harder on the penny or on each other's skin. You can also play solo by touching the pennies with one finger from each hand. You'll soon get a feel for how to change the sounds of the Friendstrument by varying pressure on the pennies.

How It Works

Your body conducts electricity. When you touch the Friendstrument's pennies, you are allowing current to flow across your skin (it's a tiny, harmless amount) and complete the circuit. This kind of circuit is used in lie detector machines. When people are lying, they sweat more, which increases the skin's conductivity and, therefore, the current flowing through the circuit, causing the pen on the lie detector's graph to jump. You can use the Friendstrument as a crude lie detector, but if you're a police officer, don't rely on it as proof of guilt or innocence.

MIXIE STICKS

Race against time to match colored sticks that snap together with magnets

Jane invented a color-matching game that uses colored markers as the playing pieces. To prepare the game, we pull the caps (which are the same color as their respective pen barrels) off ten to twelve marker pens and put them back on the wrong pens. Then, using a stopwatch, we shout "Go!" and one player races to put all the colored caps on their matching barrels as quickly as possible. We record the time it takes for each player to complete the challenge. The player who does it in the shortest amount of time is declared the winner.

The only problem with the game is that the pens are round, and they tend to roll off the table or across the floor during play. So we came up with a new set of playing pieces made from square wood, adding magnets to the ends so the pieces stick together.

THINGS YOU NEED TO MAKE MIXIE STICKS

MATERIALS

- **40- to 80-inch piece of wood,** ¾-inch square. Each Mixie Stick is made from two 2-inch pieces of wood.

- **Paintbrushes and acrylic paints**
- **Clear acrylic spray**
- **20–40 neodymium magnets,** ³⁄₁₆-inch cube. A pack of 64 costs about $20 on Amazon.

TOOLS

- **Saw.** Use a miter saw or a band saw to get square edges
- **Sandpaper,** various grits
- **Metal or plastic ruler**
- **Pencil**
- **Drill and ¼-inch drill bit**
- **Hot glue gun and hot glue sticks,** to secure magnets if needed

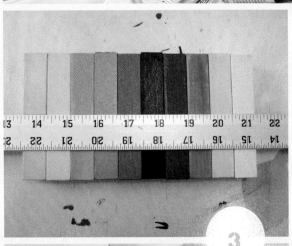

How to Make Mixie Sticks

1   Cut the wood into 4-inch lengths, as shown in the Materials List. Sand the edges so they are smooth.

2   Paint each stick a different color. When the paint dries, apply a few coats of clear acrylic spray.

3   Cut the sticks in half. Use a ruler and pencil to draw a straight line across them, then saw them in half.

4   Drill holes in the cuts ends of each Mixie Stick. Find the center point of the surface by drawing two straight lines from corner to corner using the ruler. Drill a ¼-inch hole about ½ inch deep in each end.

5   Insert the magnets into the holes. Start with two magnets stuck together. Press the stack of magnets into one of the Mixie Stick ends until the magnet in the hole is about halfway in. Then place the second stick half against the first stick half and push the halves together, but not all the way. Pull the magnets apart and use the flat of the ruler to press the magnets into the holes so that they are flush with the surface of the sticks.

Note: If the magnets come out of the hole, add a drop of hot glue to the hole and press the magnet in again.

Now it's time to play!

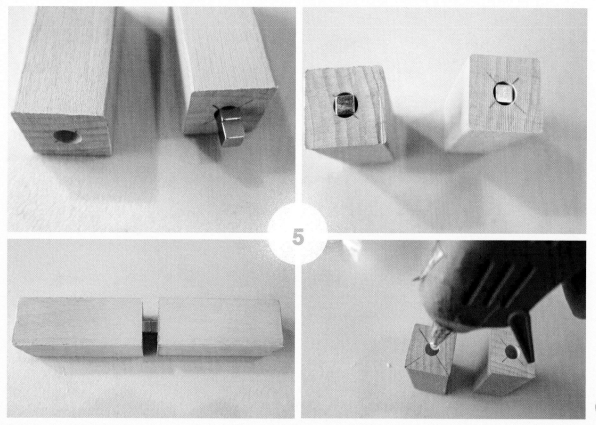

How to Play Mixie Sticks

1 Attach Mixie Stick halves together randomly. Set a stopwatch (most smartphones have one) to zero and shout "Go!"

2 When the player has rearranged the halves so that they all match, he or she shouts "Stop!" and the stopwatch is stopped. Write down the time on a score sheet and set up the Mixie Sticks for the next player.

BONUS: SUPER CHALLENGE MIXIE STICKS

Older kids and adults will enjoy this more difficult version of Mixie Sticks. Each side of the Mixie Stick is painted a different color, and there are no magnets, so you don't know which end matches to which.

Paint the sticks as follows:

Blue Red Black Green

Blue Black Green Red

Blue Green Red Black

Yellow Red Black Green

Yellow Black Green Red

Yellow Green Red Black

Blue Yellow Black Green

Blue Yellow Green Red

Blue Yellow Red Black

Blue Red Yellow Green

Blue Black Yellow Red

Blue Green Yellow Black

Blue Red Black Yellow

Blue Black Green Yellow

Blue Green Red Yellow

RETRO ARCADE
VIDEO GAME

Use free software to write your own computer game

Have you ever wondered how a video game works? How do the characters move across the screen? How does the game know when a target has been hit, or when to increase the score?

The best way to learn how a computer game works is by writing one of your own! Scratch is a wonderful programming language that was developed at the Massachusetts Institute of Technology. It's a graphical programming language that uses colored blocks that you drag and drop to build programs.

In this project you'll learn how to write a fun computer game that you can share with other people online.

THINGS YOU NEED TO MAKE A RETRO ARCADE VIDEO GAME

TOOLS

- **Scratch.** Scratch is a graphical programming language that uses colored blocks to write programs. Instead of typing out lines of computer code, you just drag and drop the colored blocks into the "Scripts Area" of Scratch and snap the blocks together. Scratch is more than just a fun way to make animations, music, games, and other interactive programs. Mitchel Resnick, the director of the MIT Scratch team at MIT's Media Lab, says that "when young people create Scratch projects, they are not just learning how to write computer programs. They are learning to think creatively, reason systematically, and work collaboratively—essential skills for success and happiness in today's world."

- **Computer.** Almost any computer made in the last five or six years will work with Scratch. You can download Scratch for Windows, Mac OS X, or Ubuntu Linux. In 2013, Scratch began offering a web-based version of Scratch, but for this project, we will use the free, downloadable version available here: scratch.mit.edu/scratch_1.4.

How to Make a Retro Arcade Video Game

A (Very) Brief Introduction to Scratch

First, let's get acquainted with Scratch. When you launch the program, it looks like this. There are four main areas. The Command Blocks Area is on the left, the Scripts Area is in the middle, the Stage is on the upper right, and the Sprite List is on the lower right (a). To learn how these different parts of Scratch work together, let's write a simple program to make the cat move.

Drag the "move 10 steps" block from the left pane into the Scripts Area. Change the 10 to 100 by clicking inside the white rectangle containing "10" and typing in the value (b).

Next, click the Control button in the upper left. Drag the block that has the green flag on it into the Scripts Area. Drag it near the top of the "move 100 steps" block. You'll see a white line appear between the two blocks. That means that they fit together like pieces in a jigsaw puzzle. Release the mouse button and they will snap together. Next, drag the block that says "stop all" and has a red stop sign next to it. Attach it to the bottom of your program (c).

Now, click the green flag in the upper right corner of the Stage. Scratchy (that's the name of the cartoon cat) will jump to the right by 100 pixels. Congratulations! You've written your first Scratch program. Of course, you've just, er, *scratched* the surface of what Scratch can do. Feel free to play around with the different command blocks to see what happens. Scratch is meant to be used in a trial-and-error fashion. (Visit makerdad.org for a link to an excellent PDF guide called *Getting Started with Scratch*.)

Now it's time to write your video game!

The game is called Dew Drop. The object is to catch blue dew drops falling from the sky while avoiding the angry magenta drops.

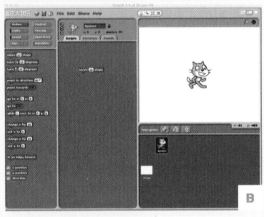

Start a new file by selecting New from the File pull-down menu (d).

PART I: CREATE THE ARTWORK

In this part of the project, we will create all the artwork for the game: the Catcher, the Dew Drops, and the backgrounds.

1 **Create the Catcher sprite.** In Scratch, an image that can move around the screen is called a sprite (a). You can use Scratchy the Cat or you can import an image or photo (you can even take a photo with your computer's camera and put yourself in the game). Scratch also has a built-in painting program that lets you create new sprites. Let's use the painting program. Click on the Costumes tab. You'll see two different costumes for Sprite1 (you'll learn more about costumes later). One is called costume1 and the other is called costume2. Click on the little X next to costume2 to delete it because we won't need it.

Click Edit and use the simple painting utility to erase Scratchy and draw your new image (or you can download the set of images we created at makerdad.org) (b).

When you are finished, click OK and name the sprite and the costume "Catcher" (c).

A

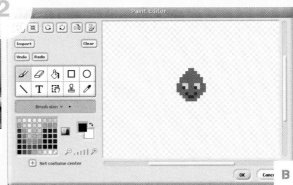

2

B

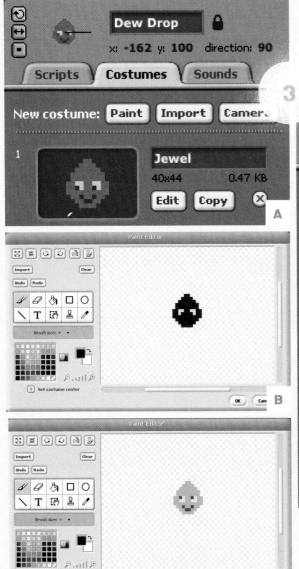

A

B

C

3

D

2 **Create the Dew Drop sprite.** (a) Click the gold star with a paintbrush on it in the Sprite List section and paint a very small icon of a dew drop. (b) We made a little blue one, shown here. When you are done name it "Drew Drop."

3 **Create costumes for the Dew Drop sprite.** A costume is exactly what it sounds like. It's a different look for a particular sprite.

We need three costumes for the Dew Drop sprite: Jewel, Thief, and Slow. To create the Jewel costume, click the Costumes tab. Name it "Jewel" (a). Now, click Copy. It will create a new costume called Jewel1. Change the name to "Thief" and click Edit.

Use the paint editor to modify the Jewel costume into an angry-looking character (b). Click OK.

Repeat the Copy-and-Edit process to make a third costume (c). Name it "Slow."

The Dew Drop sprite now has three costumes (d).

4 **Paint your Stage backgrounds.** If you've ever participated in a theatrical play, you probably know about painted backdrops. These are large painted canvas sheets that hang in the back of the stage to convey different scenes. Scratch also has backgrounds. For this game, we need two backgrounds. Get started by clicking the Stage button in the Sprite List area. Then click the Backdrops tab in the Scripts Area and click Edit to paint a background (you may also import a photo if you would rather use a photo as a background) (a). Name it "Field."

Create a new background by clicking Paint. Create some art to indicate that the game is over and name it "Boohoo" (b). When you're finished, your backgrounds will look something like this (c):

A

B

PART 2: SET UP VARIABLES

Now that we've created all the art we need for the game, it's time to set up a few variables. What's a variable? Think of it as a container with a label on it. Imagine a container that is labeled "money." If the container is empty, the value of "money" is zero. If you toss a dime into the container, the value of "money" is 10 cents. If you remove a nickel, the value becomes 5 cents. It's as simple as that.

For this game, we need three variables. One variable keeps track of how many lives a player has. Another variable keeps track of the score. And the third variable keeps track of how quickly the Dew Drops fall from the sky.

Click the Data button in the Command Blocks Area. Use the Make a Variable button to create the three variables (a), and name them "Lives," "Score," and "Drop Speed." (If the For all sprites and For this sprite only buttons are visible, make sure to click For all sprites, so the variables can be used by all the sprites in the game.) In the Command Blocks Area, make sure the Lives and Score boxes are checked (b), but don't check the Drop Speed box. That's because we want to display the Lives and Score variables in the upper left corner of the Stage, but not the Drop Speed variable.

PART 3: WRITE SCRIPTS

Now that the art and variables are finished, we can write the scripts that run the game. Don't be intimidated by the long stacks of command blocks. I'll explain how they work a step at a time.

1   **Write the start-of-game script.** Make sure the Catcher sprite is active by clicking on it in the Sprite List. Then click the Scripts tab in the Scripts Area. Drag out the commands to create the script shown.

Note: To get rid of a command that you no longer need, drag it back over to the Command Blocks Area.

Let's go through this script command by command so you understand what's going on.

The green flag command means that the script will be run when you click the green flag in the Stage. This starts the game (a).

These three orange-colored commands assign values to the three variables you created earlier. We set the Lives to 3. If you want to make the game easier, change the value to 5 or even a higher number (b).

The "show" command makes the Catcher sprite appear.

The "go to" command positions the sprite at the bottom of the screen (y = -140) at the horizontal midpoint (x = 0) (c).

The "say" command will cause your sprite to say whatever you tell it to say in the form of a comic book word balloon. You can specify how long you want the words to stay on the screen (d).

The "broadcast" command is very useful. In this case, it is broadcasting the word "Picker" to run the Picker script. We will get to that script a little later on.

The "stop" command simply means that the script should stop being executed (e).

So, to recap what this script does:

- It assigns values to the three variables used in the game.

- It causes the Catcher sprite to be displayed and positions it in the proper place on the Stage.

- It causes the Catcher sprite to say the rules of the game.

- It broadcasts the word "Picker" to randomly determine which of the three different costumes will fall from the sky.

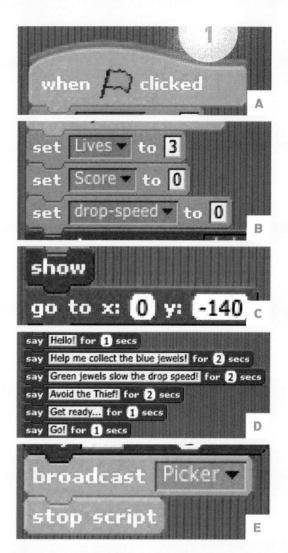

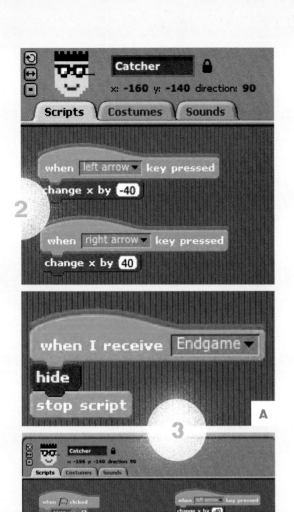

There are three more scripts that the Catcher needs, and they are very short. Two of them move the Catcher, and the third one ends the game. All three of these scripts share the same Scripts Area as the start-of-game script.

2   **Write the Catcher movement scripts.** The Catcher needs to move from side to side so it can catch Dew Drop sprites. Drag out a "when . . . key pressed" command block from the Control palette, and select "left arrow" from its pull-down menu. Then drag a "change x by" block from the Motion palette and change the number to -40. Do the same for the right arrow, using a value of 40. Test your work by using the left and right arrow keys to move the Catcher back and forth. Neat!

Note: You can copy an entire script by using the Duplicate tool, which is above the Stage.

3   **Write the end-of-game script.** This script waits for another script (which we will look at later) to broadcast the word "Endgame," and then it hides the Catcher (a).

Here are all four scripts for the Catcher as they appear in the Scripts Area for the Catcher sprite.

Now we will write five scripts for the Dew Drop sprite (b).

4   **Write the Picker script.** Start by clicking the Dew Drop sprite in the Sprite List. Now, remember how you created three different costumes for the Dew Drop sprite: Jewel, Thief, and Slow? Well, the Picker script randomly determines which of the three different costumes will fall from the sky. Let's go over it step by step (a).

The "when I receive" command is set so that when it receives the "Picker" broadcast, the rest of the script starts running (b).

The first thing the script does is check to see if the value of Lives is less than 1. If it is, then it broadcasts the words "Endgame," and the end-of-game script starts running. If the value of Lives is 1 or greater, then it executes the rest of the script. It does this by using an "if . . . else" command (c).

Here's what happens when the value of Lives is 1 or greater. It generates a random number between -210 and 210 for the horizontal position for the Dew Drop. It also assigns a value of 100 for the vertical position of the Dew Drop. In other words, this part of the script creates a Dew Drop sprite at the top of the screen and at a random horizontal location (d). (But it doesn't show the sprite yet.)

In this part of the script there are two "if . . . else" commands inside the first "if . . . else" script. This is known as "nesting" and is very common in computer programs. The script first chooses a random number between 1 and 15. If the random number it generates is 1, then it broadcasts the word "slowdown," and, as you probably know by now, there's a script elsewhere in the program that is listening for "slowdown" to be broadcast. If the random number is not 1 (that is, 2 through 15), then it generates *another* random number between 1 and 5. If it is 1, it broadcasts "Thief." Otherwise, it broadcasts "Jewel" (e).

Now we will take a look at the other four scripts in the Dew Drop sprite. Three of the scripts listen for "Jewel," "slowdown," or "Thief" to be broadcast before springing into action.

5

A

```
when I receive Jewel ▼
switch to costume Jewel ▼
show
forever
    if  < touching Catcher ▼ ? >
        hide
        change Score ▼ by 1
        change drop-speed ▼ by -1
        broadcast Picker ▼
        stop script
    else
        if  < touching edge ▼ ? >
            hide
            change Lives ▼ by -1
            change drop-speed ▼ by -1
            broadcast Picker ▼
            stop script
        else
            wait 0.1 secs
            change y by ( drop-speed + -20 )
```

B

```
when I receive Jewel ▼
switch to costume Jewel ▼
show
```

C

```
forever
    if  < touching Catcher ▼ ? >
        hide
        change Score ▼ by 1
        change drop-speed ▼ by -1
        broadcast Picker ▼
        stop script
    else
```

D

```
    else
        if  < touching edge ▼ ? >
            hide
            change Lives ▼ by -1
            change drop-speed ▼ by -1
            broadcast Picker ▼
            stop script
        else
```

E

```
        else
            wait 0.1 secs
            change y by ( drop-speed + -20 )
```

5 **Write the Jewel script.** The complete Jewel script is shown opposite. Let's break the script down into easy-to-understand chunks (a).

When the Picker script broadcasts the word "Jewel," it begins to run. The first thing it does is switch the Dew Drop sprite costume to Jewel and then show the costume (b).

The rest of the script is inside a "forever" loop. That means it will continue to run the script over and over again until an event occurs that causes another script to be run. Inside the "forever" loop is an "if…else" loop. It checks to see if the Dew Drop sprite is touching the Catcher. If it is, that means the Catcher has caught the Dew Drop. The "hide" command causes the sprite to disappear (to make it look like the Catcher has eaten or absorbed the Dew Drop) and it increases the score by 1. It also adds -1 to the drop speed so that the next Dew Drop will fall a little faster, making the game more challenging as it proceeds. Then the script broadcasts the word "Picker," causing the Picker script to run. The stop script command tells the Jewel script to stop running (c).

What's inside the "else" part of the Jewel script is another "if…else" loop! Since the script has already checked to see whether the Dew Drop has been caught by the Catcher, now it is going to check and see if the Dew Drop is touching one of the edges of the stage. And since the Dew Drops only move in one direction—from the top of the screen to the bottom of the screen—if it is touching an edge, it means it has fallen to the bottom of the screen without being caught. Again, we use the "hide" command to make it appear as though the drop has been absorbed into the ground. The penalty for not catching a Jewel Dew Drop is the loss of one life, so we change the Lives variable by -1. We also increase the drop speed, so that the next drop falls even faster. Then we broadcast the word "Picker," and stop the script from running (d).

The last part of the script deals with what to do with the Dew Drop if it has not yet been caught by the Catcher and it is not touching the bottom of the stage. It makes the Dew Drop continue to fall. It waits for a tenth of second and then changes the vertical position of the Dew Drop by -20 plus the value of the Drop Speed variable. The small white arrow at the bottom is part of the "forever" loop, signaling the script to run again from the beginning (e).

6 **Write the slowdown script.** The purpose of the slowdown script is to create a special Dew Drop that slows the drops as they fall from the sky, making them easier to catch. The slowdown script is similar to the Jewel script. (Hint: Clone the Jewel script and modify it so it matches the script shown here.)

7 **Write the Thief script.** If you catch a Thief Dew Drop by mistake, you will lose one life. The Picker script checks to make sure you have at least one life remaining. If there aren't any, the game is over!

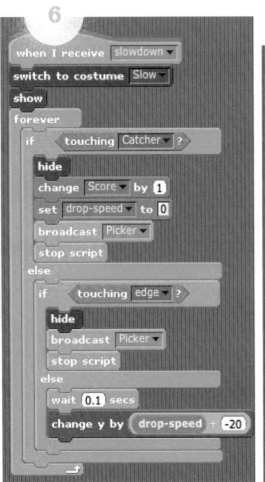

8 **Write a hide script.** This script runs every time you start a new game. Its only job is to erase any old Dew Drop sprite that isn't supposed to be seen.

9 **Write the background-switching scripts.** Click the Stage icon in the Scripts Area. We have two short scripts to write.

This script sets the background to "Field" when the game starts (a).

This script sets the background to "Boohoo" when the game is over (b).

That's it! To play the game, click the green flag.

You can play our version of the game via the link at makerdad.org.

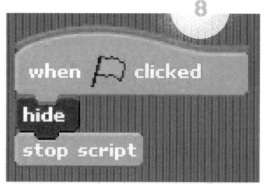

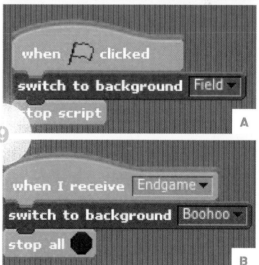

What Next?

There are many more things you can do to enhance the game. My first suggestion is to add sound effects so that every time your catcher catches or misses a Dew Drop, the game makes a sound. You can add sounds to the game by clicking on the Sound tab above the Scripts Area and selecting a sound effect. Use the Sound command in the Command Blocks Area to trigger sound effects at the appropriate times. Here's a website that has good free sound effects to use in your game: http://www.audiomicro.com/free-sound-effects.

Here are a few other ideas for enhancing the game:

1 Create a new Dew Drop that gives you an extra life.

2 Enable the player to pause the game by pressing the space bar.

3 Create a bonus round with a rain of Jewel Dew Drop sprites.

4 Create a new enemy Dew Drop sprite that shrinks the size of the Catcher.

5 Make achievement levels with new backgrounds.

Going Even Further with Scratch

There are so many things you can do with Scratch besides write games. To learn more about the capabilities of Scratch, check out *Super Scratch Programming Adventure!: Learn to Program by Making Cool Games*, published by No Starch Press (2012). There's also a $45 electronics projects board called the PicoBoard that lets you connect Scratch to the real world. It comes with a light sensor, a sound sensor, a push button, a slider, and inputs for four other sensors. Visit makerdad.org for more information.

CRAZY CARDS

Make a set of cards that seems to magically swap the cards' places with one another

Martin Gardner was a math and science writer and a magician. He wrote many entertaining books and articles about math puzzles, paradoxes, hoaxes, and magic tricks. (Some of my favorites are *Perplexing Puzzles and Tantalizing Teasers, Martin Gardner's Science Magic: Tricks and Puzzles, Aha! Gotcha: Paradoxes to Puzzle and Delight, Martin Gardner's Table Magic,* and *Entertaining Science Experiments with Everyday Objects.*) Gardner once performed a wonderful card trick for another writer named Donald Simanek, who wrote about the trick in *MAKE* magazine, which is where I first learned about it. The trick consists of four playing cards—two red cards and two black cards. The cards have holes through them, and there's a bolt and a nut through the holes, so that the order of the cards—red, black, red, black—can't be changed without removing the bolt. But the deck has a special quality: if you rotate the top two cards all the way around the bolt, the order of the cards is changed to red, red, black, black. It's an amazing trick and no one we've shown it to has ever figured it out.

Here is an easy-to-construct version of Gardner's trick, which uses a thumbtack and a small piece of wood in place of a nut and bolt, and rectangular pieces of cardboard instead of playing cards.

MATERIALS

- **Cardstock.** Enough to make four cards, approximately 2¼ in. × 4 in. We used a cardboard pencil box for our cards. A frozen pizza box or regular playing cards will work, too.
- **Thumbtack**
- **Small dowel or scrap wood,** thick enough to hold the point of the thumbtack so it doesn't protrude from the other end
- **Markers, stickers, or rubber stamps**

TOOLS

- **Scissors**
- **Metal or plastic ruler**
- **Pencil**

How to Make Crazy Cards

1 Cut out four cards from the cardstock with scissors. Make sure they are all the same size.

2 Poke a hole through the cards. Arrange the cards in a stack. Use a ruler and a pencil to make a dot along the centerline of the top card and 1¼ inches from a short edge. Poke a hole through all four cards with the thumbtack.

3 Cut curved paths on two of the cards. Draw and cut the paths shown here on two of the cards. (You don't need to draw the smiley face—we added it to help with the next step.)

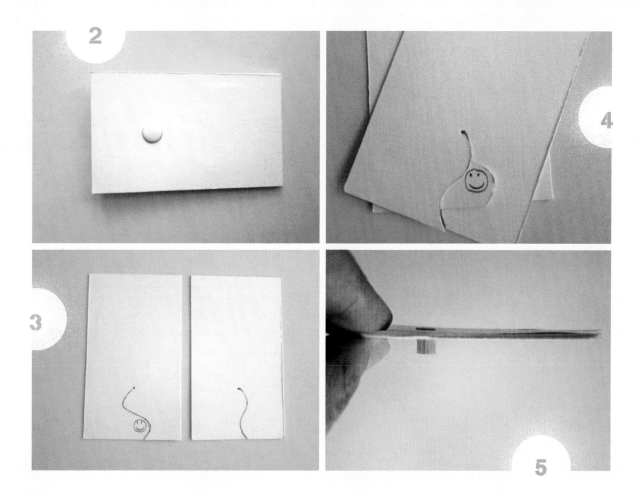

4   **Arrange the two cut cards.** Put the card with the smiley face on the bottom. Slip the tab with the smiley face through the cut path on the top card. Then straighten the cards and sandwich them between the other two (uncut) cards.

5   **Pin the cards together.** Insert the thumbtack through the holes. Push the small piece of wood over the point of the pin.

6   **Decorate the cards.** Using two colors, make symbols on the cards so you can tell them apart. We used the rubber stamps we made on page 86 to decorate the cards with green and pink stars.

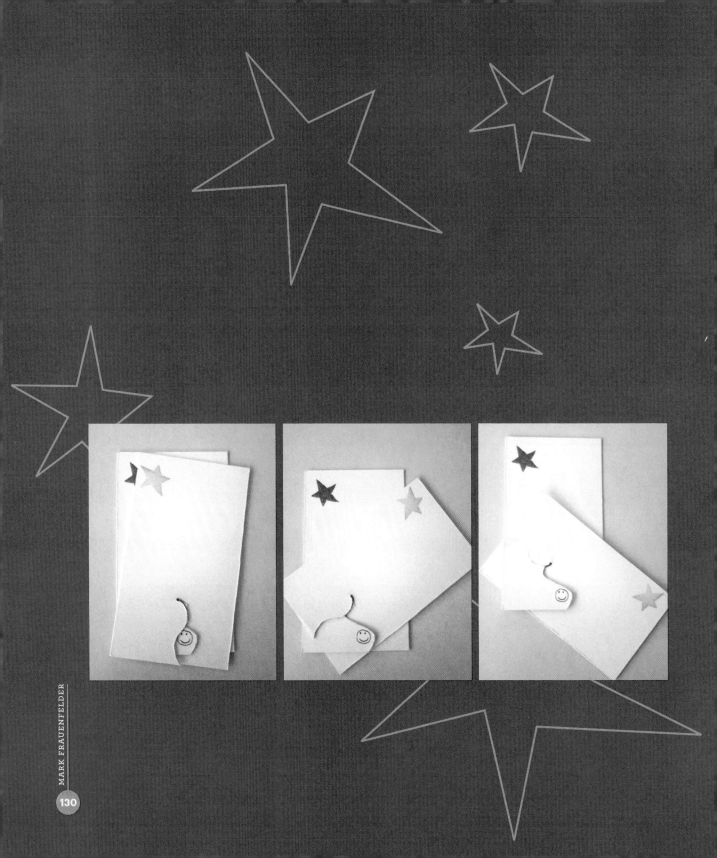

How to Use Crazy Cards

It's very easy to use Crazy Cards. They work automatically. All you have to do is rotate the top two cards, and the middle cards will swap locations in the stack.

How does it work? This series of photos of the two middle cards reveals the secret. Notice how in the first photo, the green card is on top. As the green card rotates clockwise, the tab with the smiley face (which is on the pink card) slides over the top of the green card. As the green card continues to rotate, it slides under the pink card. When the green card is fully rotated, it is now under the pink card. To put it back on top, just rotate it again!

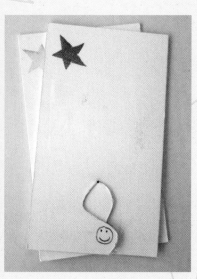

LUNCH BOX GUITAR

*Make a very playable and adorable musical
instrument from a metal lunch box*

We have a couple of guitars around the house, but my kids aren't interested in them. When I made a cigar box guitar, however, they were attracted to its whimsical design. After picking it up and strumming it, they were delighted to discover how easy it was to play, thanks to the fact that it has only three strings and uses open tuning.

I've been making guitars out of cigar boxes for a few years now, and I'm still surprised at how good they sound. Many famous guitarists, such as Howlin' Wolf and Jimi Hendrix, got their start on homemade cigar box guitars.

A lot of craft books for kids have how-to projects for "musical instruments," but they are often made from cardboard and rubber bands and they sound awful. This lunch box guitar is a real musical instrument that will last for years.

If your daughter is twelve or older, she can probably complete most of the steps on her own, with your guidance. If she is younger, she will enjoy sanding and decorating the instrument.

Please read all the instructions before buying the materials and tools, because you'll have a better feel for exactly what you'll need.

THINGS YOU NEED TO MAKE A LUNCH BOX GUITAR

MATERIALS

- **27- to 36-inch length of 1 × 2 wood, such as maple.** (Note: a 1 × 2 is actually ¾ in. × 1½ in. That's because the wood is 1 in. × 2 in. in its rough form, but after it has been planed and dried and offered for sale, the actual size has been reduced.)
- **Metal lunch box**
- **Masking tape**
- **Box of toothpicks.** Flat or square toothpicks are better for frets than round toothpicks because they will stay glued to the neck.
- **Three 1-inch wood screws.** We like coarse-thread drywall screws, but you can use what's around your house.
- **Acrylic paints,** for painting fret dots and decorating the guitar
- **High-gloss polyurethane spray paint**
- **3 tuning pegs, like SKU GTM21 from elderly.com.** The tuning pegs come in a set of six for $11.25.

- **A set of six electric guitar strings.** Any gauge will do.
- **Wooden barbecue skewer**
- **Pencil stub**

TOOLS

- **Band saw or hand saw**
- **Square**
- **Ruler**
- **Pencil**
- **Rotary cutting tool,** such as a Dremel, tin snips, or a nibbler
- **Drill and bits.** A drill press is best, but a hand drill will do.
- **¾-inch diameter spade bit**
- **File**
- **Sandpaper,** various grits
- **Gel-style superglue**
- **Nail clippers**
- **Surform Shaver.** They cost a few bucks. Here's the one to get: http://goo.gl/qgIOt.
- **Woodworking clamps**
- **Awl, nail, or pushpin**
- **Plastic bag,** large enough for the lunch box to fit inside
- **Clear tape**
- **Small Phillips-head screwdriver**

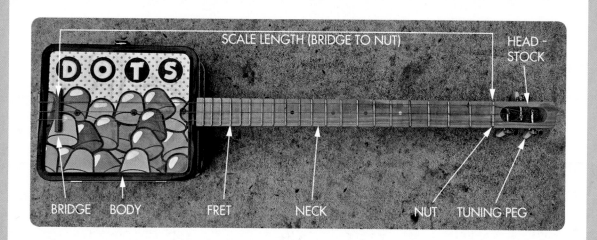

ANATOMY OF A LUNCH BOX GUITAR

Throughout these instructions, I'll be talking about different components of the lunch box guitar, such as the frets, nut, bridge, and so on. If you aren't familiar with guitar anatomy, refer to the photograph above as you go along.

How to Make a Lunch Box Guitar

1 **Select the wood for the neck carefully.** It's important to use a 1 × 2 that is very flat and straight. You don't want it to be bowed or twisted. When you and your daughter go to the lumber store, take your time and select the best piece of wood you can find. Avoid anything with knots. Hold one end up to your eye, close the other eye, and look down its length. That way you will be able to quickly spot warps and twists. Avoid soft wood like pine, because the tension of the guitar strings could cause it to bend. (It's probably not a big deal with three strings, but it's better to be safe and go for a hard wood like maple or oak.)

2 **Cut the wood to length.** We recommend cutting the 1 × 2 to a length between 27 and 32 inches. If you have a miter box like the one shown above, you can make a nice square cut.

3 **Remove a ⅛-inch layer of wood from one end of the neck** (a). The reason you want to do this is to ensure that the surface of the neck is above the surface of the lunch box when you attach them together (you'll see why later). In the photo, we've penciled in the portion you need to remove (b). The lunch box we used was 8 inches long, so we removed a 7-inch-long piece of material. Use a band saw or hand saw to first make the ⅛-inch-deep cut, followed by the 7-inch-long cut (c). Don't worry if the resulting cut isn't pretty—it will remain hidden inside the lunch box.

SAFETY

Should you allow your daughter to use a power tool, such as a band saw? A band saw, and even a handsaw, can give you a nasty cut if you aren't careful. If your daughter has the fine motor skills needed to use a saw, let her make the cuts, but monitor her. Be prepared to hit the off button on a second's notice. Make sure you are both wearing safety goggles. If your daughter has long hair, get it out of the way of moving machinery by covering her hair in a hair net or a hat.

4 **Make a rectangular hole in the lunch box for the guitar neck.** Prepare the lunch box by covering the short ends with masking tape as shown (a). This will allow you to make measurement marks and will also keep the paint from getting scratched off if a tool slips. Find the midpoint of the short ends and mark it with a pencil. On the right side of the lunch box use a square, a ruler, and a pencil to draw a 1½ in. × ⅝ in. rectangular hole (b). Use tin snips, a nibbler, or a rotary cutting tool (like a Dremel tool) to make two parallel cuts in the lid as shown (c). Just bend the resulting flap against the top of the lid as shown. Make a similar cut in the bottom part of the lunch box and fold the flap down (d).

5 **Close the lunch box and stick the neck in the hole you cut to make sure it fits.** If the hole is too small, use your snips or Dremel to make the hole a bit larger.

6 **Cut the hole for the tuning pegs.** Now let's turn our attention to the other end of the neck, also known as the headstock (the end that you did not remove a slice from). Use the square to measure and mark the centerline of the neck. Then make two pencil marks (a): the first mark 1 inch from the end of the neck, and the second mark 3 inches from the end of the neck (b). Drill holes at both of these pencil marks with a ¾-inch diameter spade bit (c). Now, you need to remove the wood between the two holes to form an elongated hole. We accomplished this by using the spade bit to drill additional holes in between the first two holes we drilled (d).

After that use a Dremel tool or a file and sandpaper to clean up the hole (e).

7   **Sand the fretboard surface of the neck.** Now that you have your sandpaper out, it's a good time to give the surface of the neck a good sanding to get rid of bumps and roughness. Wrap the sandpaper around a block of wood to keep the surface as dead flat as possible.

8   **Mark the frets.** Fret placement is very important. If you get it wrong, you will never be able to tune the guitar properly. You can calculate where to place the frets in one of two ways. Both ways require you to begin by deciding on the length of the neck. This is simply the distance between the guitar's bridge and the front edge of the nut (look at the Anatomy of a Lunch Box Guitar photo on page 135). On the guitar we made, the bridge-to-nut length is 23.9 inches.

    Fret placement method #1: If you wish, you and your daughter can use math to determine the fret locations. This website does a good job of explaining how: liutaiomottola.com/formulae/fret.htm. (It's a tempered scale, such as the kind a guitar uses—there are twelve tones between octaves, and the tones vary as a function of the twelfth root of two.)

    Fret placement method #2: The easier way to locate your fret marks is to use an online fret position calculator. Simply enter the scale length and the number of frets you want on your guitar (twenty or twenty-one is plenty), and let the program crunch the numbers. The best one is on Stewart-MacDonald's website: www.stewmac.com/freeinfo/Fretting/i-fretcalc.html. (Stewart-MacDonald is also a good place to buy guitar parts like tuning pegs and fret wire.) Be sure to measure the location of each fret from the nut. Don't measure from fret to fret, because measurement errors will accumulate and really screw up the location of the frets as you move down the neck. When drawing the pencil marks, use a square to ensure that the frets are parallel with one another and perpendicular to the neck.

9   **Glue the toothpicks over the fret marks.** A gel-style superglue works well because it dries quickly and, unlike regular nonviscous superglue, it won't soak into the wood and disappear before it has a chance to stick. Squirt a thin bead of glue over the pencil mark and lay the toothpick over it. You can use your square to make sure the toothpick stays at a 90-degree angle to the neck. Press down for about 20–30 seconds before moving on to the next fret.

10 **Snip off the ends of the toothpicks.** Once all the toothpicks have been glued on, use a pair of nail clippers to snip off the ends of the toothpicks as close to the edge of the neck as possible.

11 **Sand the toothpicks.** Use a fairly fine-grit sandpaper (P180 is about right) wrapped around a block of wood to sand down the toothpicks to about two-thirds their original thickness. Next, you need to smooth down the ends of the toothpicks. If you have a "real" guitar handy, inspect the way the frets are shaped at the edges. They are angled down so that your fingers don't catch on them as you move your hand up and down the neck. Use the sandpaper to make nice smooth angles on both ends of all the toothpicks.

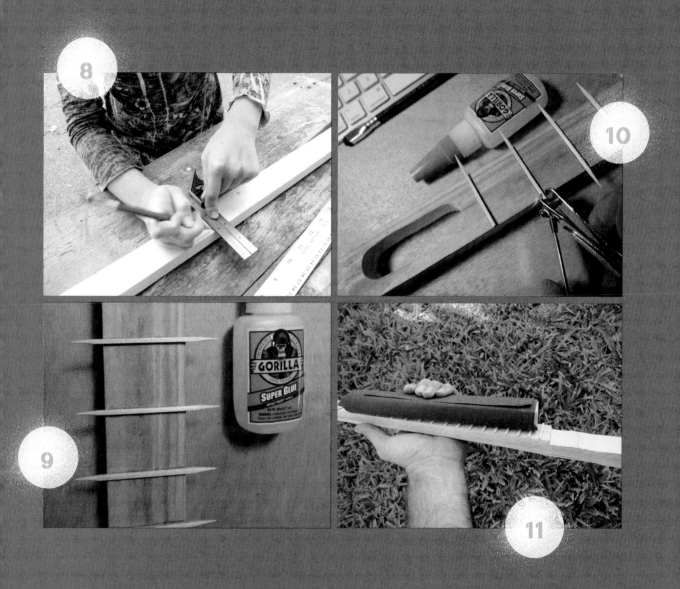

12 **Drill holes for the tuning pegs.** Since the mounting holes for tuning pegs aren't uniform from manufacturer to manufacturer, we can't tell you exactly where to drill the holes. Hold the pegs against the neck to figure out where to position them on the neck. Ensure that when the tuning pegs are mounted, the little gear is pointing down (toward the body). Use a ¼-inch bit to drill one side of the neck with one hole for one tuning peg and two holes in the other side of the neck for the other two pegs as shown in the photo above. Use a 1/16-inch bit to drill pilot holes for the mounting screws. Use sandpaper to clean up the holes.

13 **Smooth the edges along the length of the neck.** This is where the $3 Surform tool comes into play. You'll use it to round the corners along the length of the neck, changing the cross section from a rectangular shape to a U shape. Use your judgment to decide when the edges are sufficiently rounded down. You and your daughter should hold the neck and pretend to play the guitar to get a feel for how much more material needs to be shaved away. Once you're happy with the shape, finish with sandpaper.

14 **Mount the neck to the lunch box.** Insert the neck into the notch you cut in the lid of the lunch box. Use the clamps and the square to make sure the neck is flush against the lid and isn't crooked. The fretboard surface should be at a higher level than the top of the lunch box lid. If it isn't, you need to sand more wood from the part of the neck that's clamped to the lunch box. This will ensure sufficient clearance between the strings and the lunch box. (The first time I made a cigar box guitar, I neglected to do this and learned my lesson after I added strings and tried to play it!)

With the neck still clamped to the lid, use an awl to punch three holes in the lunch box lid along the centerline of the neck. Then drill the holes with a 1/16-inch bit. The holes can go all the way through the wood. Screw 1-inch fasteners (such as coarse-thread drywall screws) into the holes and screw them down fairly tight. The photo below shows the screw heads after we touched them up with gumdrop-colored paint. Step back and take a look at what you've accomplished so far. It's starting to look like a guitar, isn't it?

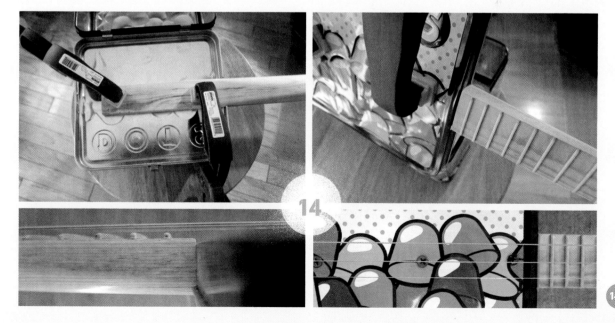

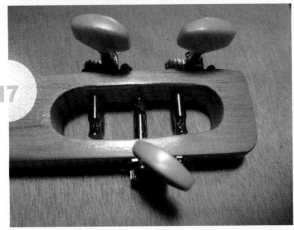

15 **Paint fret dots.** You can make fret dots with colored markers or paint. We had some Liquitex acrylic paint so we used that. Traditionally, the dots are placed on the third, fifth, seventh, ninth, and twelfth spaces between the frets on the neck (starting from the headstock and counting toward the body). You and your daughter might want to paint flowers, chibi characters, or other symbols instead of dots. She can even use stick-ers (not puffy ones) or decals.

16 **Apply varnish to the neck.** This step is optional, but it really makes your guitar look nice, and it also makes the toothpick frets stronger. Cover the lunch box with a plastic bag and tape. Go outside with a spray can of high-gloss poly-urethane. Spray on several coats, allowing 10–15 minutes drying time between applications (it might take longer, depending on the weather). You can lightly sand the neck with a fine-grit sandpaper between applications. We applied five coats to the guitar we built.

17 **Attach the tuning pegs.** Use the small screws supplied with the tuning pegs to attach them to the neck.

18 **Punch string holes in the lunch box.** With the awl or a hammer and a sharp nail, punch three small holes in the lid of the box. The middle hole should be on the centerline of the neck, and the other two holes should be ½ inch on either side of the middle hole.

19 **String the guitar and add the nut, saddle, and strain relief for the strings.** If you've never put new strings on a guitar, go online to see how it's done. For an excellent guide, search YouTube for "How to String an Electric Guitar for Dummies." When the strings are no longer slack, you'll need to insert three things under the strings: a piece of barbecue skewer (or a material with similar dimensions, such as a piece of coat hanger wire) on the pencil line you drew for the nut, a pencil stub on the lunch box lid, and another piece of skewer next to the three holes you punch in the previous step (see step 18 photo).

20 **Set the scale and tune the guitar.** Remember the length you decided on? That's how far away the pencil stub (your bridge) should be away from the barbecue skewer (your nut). Slide the pencil into position. You are going to tune the guitar using open tuning. It's easy: First, tighten the top string (the first string your thumb hits on a downstroke) until you are pleased with the sound. (Don't make it so tight that the string will snap, though!) Then put your finger on the seventh fret position and pluck it. That's what the middle string should sound like when it is plucked without fretting it. Then fret the middle string on the fifth fret position and adjust the third string to match it. Since the strings are new and unstretched, you will have to retune it for a day or two until the strings settle in.

Finally, you'll want to fine-tune the guitar by angling the pencil. Place your finger on the middle string, directly over the twelfth toothpick, but don't press the string down all the way to the fretboard. Pluck it. You should hear a clear sound. If you don't, you will need to slide the pencil up or down a little until this harmonic rings clear. Next, place your finger over the twelfth toothpick of one of the other two strings and listen for the harmonic. If you don't get it, then tilt the pencil stub very slightly up or down (without changing the position of the pencil location under the middle string) until you get the harmonic. Once you've got it nailed, retune the guitar.

21 **Check for high spots on the toothpicks.** Pluck each string on every fret. If you get a flat sound, a buzz, or a dead sound, it means a toothpick higher up the neck is not clearing the string. Take a close look to see which proud toothpick is the culprit. Once you spot it, teach it a lesson with a bit of sandpaper.

22 **Tighten the box to eliminate rattling sounds.** If the guitar rattles or buzzes when you play it, it could mean that the handle is vibrating or the lid is not clamped on tightly enough. We drilled a hole through the handle of the lunch box and tightened it down with a screw. If the lid is giving you problems, you might want to add a bit of rubbery foam inside the box where the lid meets the edge of the box.

23 **Learn to play.** Congratulations—you've built a working three-string guitar! Have fun strumming it and getting to know it. You and your daughter can make pleasant music just by fretting all three strings along any fret (especially frets three and five). To learn how to play really fun bluesy music on it, we highly recommend watching the videos of two accomplished cigar box musicians: Shane Speal and Keni Lee Burgess. You can join Cigar Box Nation (cigarboxnation.com) for free and click the "How to Play Cigar Box Guitar" link on the front page of the website.

Here's a Hello Kitty lunch box guitar
I made for my four-year-old niece for Christmas.

SEVEN-PIECE PUZZLE CUBE

When I was a kid, my parents gave me a puzzle for Christmas. It was a red plastic cube built from seven pieces (each with a different shape) called Soma. The object of the puzzle was to take the cube apart and put it back together. I thought it would be a snap to solve. But I sat at the kitchen counter for more than an hour trying to make the cube again. Maddeningly, the booklet that came with the Soma cube said that there were "240 simple ways and 1,105,920 mathematically different ways" that the seven pieces could be put together to form a cube. I was having trouble finding just one way to solve the puzzle. Sometimes I would get very close to solving it, but the last piece wouldn't be the shape I needed. When I finally put the pieces together to form a cube, I jumped for joy. After that, I was hooked on the cube for several months. I even subscribed to the Soma newsletter, published by Parker Brothers, the manufacturer of the Soma cube. (Unfortunately, the newsletter lasted only four issues.)

Soma was invented in the early 1930s by a Danish scientist and puzzle maker named Piet Hein. The idea came to him while he was listening to a lecture by the great physicist Werner Heisenberg, who was discussing quantum mechanics. At one point in the lecture, Heisenberg mentioned something about slicing space into cubes, and Hein imagined the Soma cube. He began selling them (made out of rosewood), and they were a hit in Europe but remained relatively unknown in the United States until 1969, when Parker Brothers made the plastic version. In this project, we'll show you how to make a Soma-style cube out of twenty-seven small cubes of wood. After you build it and make a cube, we'll show you some other shapes that you can make with the pieces.

MATERIALS

- **27 wooden craft cubes.** We bought a bag of fifty ½-inch cubes, but a larger dimension would work just as well.
- **Wood glue**
- **Paintbrushes and acrylic paints (optional)**

How to Make a Seven-Piece Puzzle Cube

1 Glue together the pieces into seven shapes. Six of the pieces are made from four craft cubes each, and the seventh piece is made from three craft cubes. None of the seven pieces are the same.

2 Paint the pieces, if you wish.

Things to Make with the Puzzle Cube

The first thing you should try to make with the pieces is a cube. If you have trouble, don't get discouraged. You'll eventually succeed! If you really get stuck, use the photo here as a reference.

On the opposite page are a few other shapes you can build. If you search online for "soma cube" you'll find dozens of other shapes to make. Jane came up with the shape shown in the photo at the beginning of this project. She says it's a juice pack with a straw. If you play with your cubes enough, you will be able to memorize their shapes and solve problems in your head!

RAINBOW POPS

Colorful frozen desserts

The Popsicle was invented by accident in 1905 by an eleven-year-old boy named Frank Epperson. He'd been mixing together ingredients to make soda pop and left the drink—with the stirring stick in the glass—on the porch overnight. The next morning he discovered that the cold temperature had frozen his drink. He also discovered that it was delicious. As an adult, Epperson sold his creation (he combined the words "pop" and "icicle" to come up with the name "Popsicle") at an amusement park in Northern California.

Thanks to Epperson, Popsicles are now a treat found around the world. They come in many different flavors (the most popular is orange) and a variety of shapes. In this project, we'll show you how to make your own ice pops in molds made from toys around your house.

MATERIALS

- **Shapes to make molds from.** Use any object that has a smooth shape and doesn't have small features that extend out of the main shape. An egg (real or fake) is good. So are vinyl toys, pieces of fruit, or small bottles. Whatever you use, it should be something that's easy to remove from the rubber mold. For instance, a plastic doll with arms and legs is not suitable.

- **Silicone molding compound.** Use a food-grade molding compound. We used EasyMold (the same stuff we used in the Soap Shapes project on page 32).

- **Paper towels**

- **Paper or plastic cups**

- **Juice of various colors**

- **Wooden craft sticks.** These look just like Popsicle sticks.

- **Tape (clear or masking)**

TOOLS

- **Craft knife**

- **Rubber bands**

- **Binder clip**

- **Freezer**

How to Make Rainbow Pops

1   Select a suitable object to cast. Here, we are using a glass egg. It's 2¾ inches tall. Estimate how much molding compound you'll need to cover the surface of the object with a layer about ⅓ inch thick.

2   Cover your object with the molding compound. Mix two equal amounts of the molding compound and cover your object. You need to work quickly because the compound gets too hard to work with after a couple of minutes. Let it harden completely.

3   Remove the object from the mold. It was easy to remove the small drinking glass from the mold. The egg was harder to remove, and we had to cut a slit in the rubber with a craft knife.

4 Prepare the mold. Wash the mold with soap and water, rinse thoroughly, and dry with a paper towel. Place the mold in a plastic or paper cup and use paper towels to stabilize the mold and to elevate the top of the mold so it is flush with the top of the cup. If you had to cut a slit in the mold to remove the object, carefully wrap the mold with a couple of rubber bands.

5 Pour in the juice. If you want a single-colored pop, pour juice to nearly the top of the mold (leave a little space to allow for expansion of the liquid when it freezes). If you want a multicolored pop, pour in an inch or so of juice.

6 Make a Popsicle stick stabilizer. Tape two craft sticks together with tape as shown. Leave a gap between the sticks. Keep the popsicle stick from falling by attaching a binder clip as shown.

7 Insert the stick into the mold. There should be about 1 inch of space between the bottom of the stick and the bottom of the pop mold (think of the way a store-bought Popsicle looks). Now put the setup in the freezer and don't disturb it for a few hours.

8 Add more layers of juice. Use a different color of juice each time. If you only have two colors, you can alternate them for a two-toned striped pop. Let each layer freeze completely (a couple of hours should do the trick) before adding another layer.

9 Remove the ice pop from the mold. After pouring the final layer, let the pop freeze for a couple of hours before pulling it out of the mold. Don't pull on the stick too hard or it might come loose from the pop. If the pop doesn't come out easily, press the rubber mold gently on the sides and bottom to squeeze it out.

Enjoy!

ASTRO
ICE CREAM

A fluffy, crunchy ice cream treat that never melts

If you've ever visited a museum gift shop, chances are you have seen those plastic foil packets of "astronaut ice cream" for sale. If you've tried it, you know that not only does it taste amazingly good—crunchy, creamy, and melt-in-your-mouth—but it also is made from real ice cream that has been freeze-dried.

Freeze-drying is a process that was developed in World War II as a way to preserve medical supplies, but soon after, food processors began using it to preserve food as well. The idea behind freeze-drying is to remove the water from foods in such a way that when water is re-added to the dehydrated food it quickly reconstitutes into its original form. Backpackers who want to travel as lightly as possible carry freeze-dried food with them because it's very lightweight and cooks quickly.

The equipment for freeze-drying is expensive because it requires a vacuum chamber, a powerful pump to remove the air from the chamber, and a means to lower the temperature of the food well below freezing. We love astronaut ice cream so much that we wanted to find a way to make it at home, so my daughters and I started looking around for other ways to create a crunchy, fluffy treat that was made from the same ingredients used in ice cream. After much trial and error involving whipped cream dispensers and homemade Dremel tool attachments designed to whip the liquid ice cream into a permanent froth, we stumbled on a simple way to make astronaut ice cream at home that tastes remarkably like the commercial version. Follow the recipe below to make Neapolitan astronaut ice cream and then you will be ready for liftoff.

MATERIALS

- **6 ounces of milk.** We used whole milk, but skim or low-fat milk ought to be fine.
- **3 tablespoons powdered glucose.** Sometimes it is called dextrose. We used the powdered version, but it also comes as a liquid. You can order it online or get it at a cake decoration supply shop or health food store.
- **1 egg white**
- **⅛ teaspoon vanilla extract**
- **1-inch square of dark chocolate**
- **1–2 large strawberries**

TOOLS

- **Electric whisk.** It looks like an eggbeater, but it's motorized and spins quickly.
- **Microwave**
- **3 microwave-safe mixing bowls**
- **Measuring cups and spoons**
- **Aluminum foil**
- **Cookie sheet**
- **Toaster oven,** food dehydrator, or oven that can be set to 175 degrees
- **Ziploc bag,** to store the ice cream in the freezer

How to Make Astro Ice Cream

The secret to making fluffy, crunchy astronaut ice cream is to get the *right kind of foam*, one that is both stable and has enough structural integrity to stand up to the dehydration process. In the following steps we'll show you how to do it successfully. The following recipe yields a good snack for three people.

PART 1: MAKE THE ICE CREAM MIXTURE

1. Add the milk, glucose, and egg white to a mixing bowl and blend with the whisk. Thirty seconds or so should do the trick.

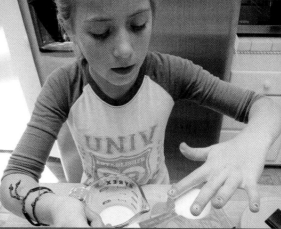
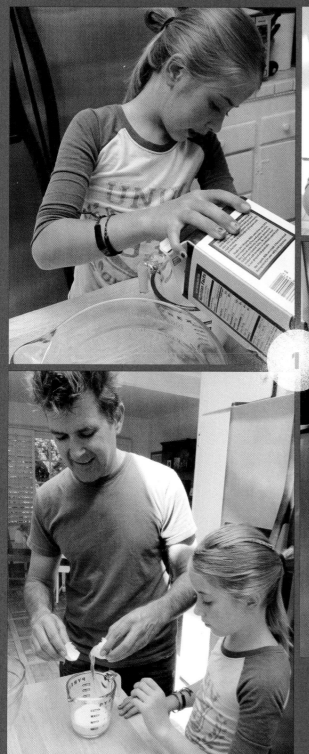

2 Microwave the mixture for 30 seconds.

3 Divide the mixture into the three separate mixing bowls. That way, you'll have chocolate, vanilla, and strawberry ice cream.

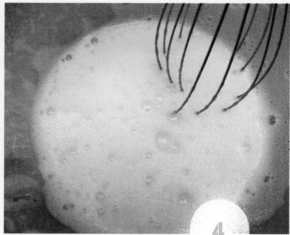

PART 2: MAKE THE VANILLA FOAM

1   Add the vanilla to one of the mixing bowls with the ice cream mixture.

2   Blend the mixture with the whisk for at least a minute; try to build up as much foam as possible.

3   Microwave the mixture for 20 seconds.

4   Examine the foam. At this point, there should be quite a bit of foam in the mixing bowl. That's a good sign, but we need to make sure it's the right kind of foam. There's the "first foam" that will collapse into a gross puddle of goo when you dehydrate it, and there's the stable "final foam" that will hold up to the 6- to 8-hour drying process. Here's how to tell the difference: Scoop up a spoonful of foam from the bowl and look at what happens to the foam in the bowl. Does the hole remain, as if you'd removed a spadeful of dirt from the ground? If so, then you've got the right kind of foam! You can move to the next step. If the hole disappears (as if you scooped up a spoonful of water) then you've got "first foam." Don't despair! Just repeat steps 2 and 3 until you get "final foam."

5   Set the bowl aside.

PART 3: MAKE THE CHOCOLATE FOAM

1 Break up a 1-inch square piece of chocolate into one of the two remaining mixing bowls.

2 Microwave the mixture for 20 seconds.

3 Blend the mixture with the whisk for at least a minute; try to build up as much foam as possible.

4 Microwave the mixture for 20 seconds.

5 Examine the foam, as you did for the vanilla mixture. From our experience, the chocolate foam is a little harder to prepare than the vanilla or strawberry. You may have to repeat steps 3 and 4 several times. But note that it is possible to go too far in an attempt to get the "final foam." If after three or four blend and nuke cycles you still aren't getting "final foam," toss the batch and start over.

6 Set the bowl aside.

3

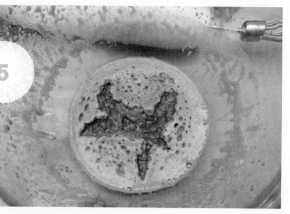

5

PART 4: MAKE THE STRAWBERRY FOAM

1. Chop up one or two strawberries and put them in the remaining mixing bowl.

2. Microwave the mixture for 20 seconds.

3. Blend the mixture with the whisk for at least a minute; try to build up as much foam as possible.

4. Microwave the mixture for 20 seconds.

5. Examine the foam. There's a very good chance it will be ready at this point. In my experience, the strawberry foam sets more quickly than chocolate or vanilla. My theory is that the natural pectin in the strawberry mixed with the glucose causes the mixture to thicken quickly. (When heated, pectin, sugar, and water combine to form a 3-D macro-molecular gel, which is what gives thickness to jam and jelly.) If you aren't seeing this happening, give it another zap in the microwave for 15–20 seconds.

6. Set the bowl aside.

PART 5: DEHYDRATE THE FLAVORED MIXTURES

1 **Preheat the oven to 175 degrees Fahrenheit.** We have a convection toaster oven, which seems to be ideal for this project. If you are using a food dehydrator, turn it on.

2 **Lay a 10-inch strip of aluminum foil on a cookie sheet.**

3 **Scoop the foam onto the foil, one long flavored row at a time.** We find that it's better not to let the rows touch one another because you want as much surface area as possible for rapid and even dehydration.

4 **Insert the cookie sheet with the rows of foam into the oven or dehydrator.**

5 **Check the process every few hours.** Press the foam gently with a spoon. If it feels spongy, let it dry for a few more hours and check again.

6 **Remove the ice cream from the foil.** Once the ice cream is completely dry, it becomes flaky and fragile. Carefully peel the foil away. The ice cream will break into pieces, but that's normal.

7 **Put the pieces into a Ziploc bag and freeze.** The dried ice cream is *hygroscopic,* which means it is able to absorb moisture from the air. If you leave your astronaut ice cream out for just an hour, it will start to get mushy! So either eat it right away or put it in a plastic bag and freeze it until you are ready to eat it.

Now that you know how to make your own astronaut ice cream, why not try some other flavors besides chocolate, vanilla, and strawberry?

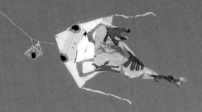

KITE VIDEO CAMERA

Shoot video from the sky

How would you like to be able to shoot video from 100 feet above your neighborhood, or at the park or beach? Well, it's easy, and you don't have to fly in an airplane or ride in a hot air balloon. Just put together this device and tie it to a kite string and send it aloft. You'll be able to take amazing video shots with it that will impress your friends. The key to taking videos from a kite is mounting the camera in a way that keeps it relatively stable while the kite is bobbling around. We will make a Picavet (named after its early nineteenth-century inventor) that keeps the camera at the same angle even though the angle of the kite string changes constantly.

THINGS YOU NEED TO MAKE A KITE VIDEO CAMERA

MATERIALS

- **Wood,** 4 inches square and ¼ inch thick

- **Clear acrylic spray**
- **4 small jewelry screw eyes.** The penny is here for size comparison.

- **5-foot string or fishing line**
- **Metal washer,** ½-inch diameter
- **2 paper clips**

- **Metal snap hair clip**

- **Key chain video camera.** Search Amazon or eBay for "key chain video camera." You should be able to buy one for $15 or less.

- **1 GB microSD card.** It costs about $7.
- **Kite and kite line**
- **Masking tape**

TOOLS

- **Computer and printer**
- **Scissors**
- **Pushpin**
- **Drill**
- **¾-inch spade bit**

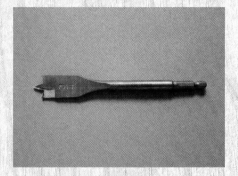

- **Rat-tail file or rotary tool with sanding drum**
- **Sandpaper,** various grits
- **Needle-nose pliers**

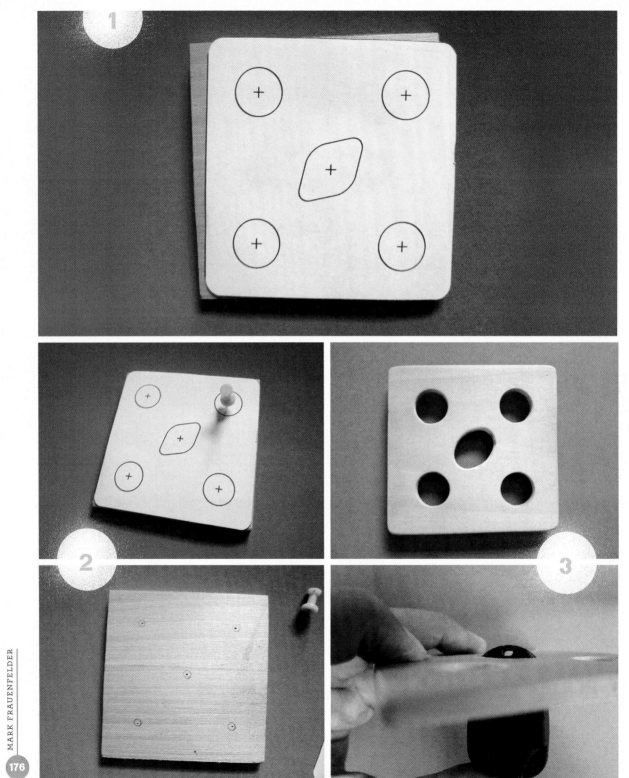

How to Make a Kite Video Camera

1   Print out the Picavet frame template. Download the drill-hole template from makerdad.org and print it out. Cut out the outline with scissors.

2   Make the drill holes. Place the template over the 4-inch square of wood and make holes in the five crosshairs with a pushpin. Remove the template and drill ¾-inch-diameter holes in all five marked spots.

3   Widen the middle hole. Use a rat-tail file or Dremel-type tool with a sanding drum to widen the middle hole as shown. You want to make the hole wide enough that when you insert the camera into the hole, the key ring hole is slightly above the top surface of the hole as shown. Use sandpaper to smooth the holes and corners of the wood and spray with clear acrylic.

4   Screw the jewelry screw eyes into the four corners of the wood. Use the needle-nose pliers to press the sharp point of the screw eyes into the wood and screw them down. Make sure the gap in the loop of the screw eye is below the surface of the wood (as shown). This will prevent the string (or fishing line) from slipping through the gap. Note the orientation of the screw eyes—they are all aligned in the same direction.

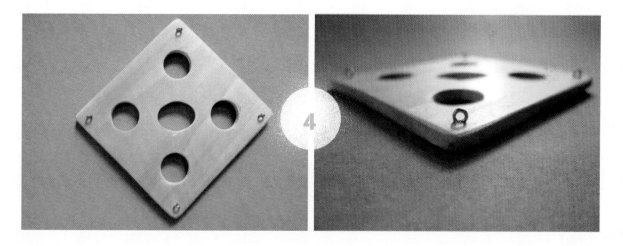

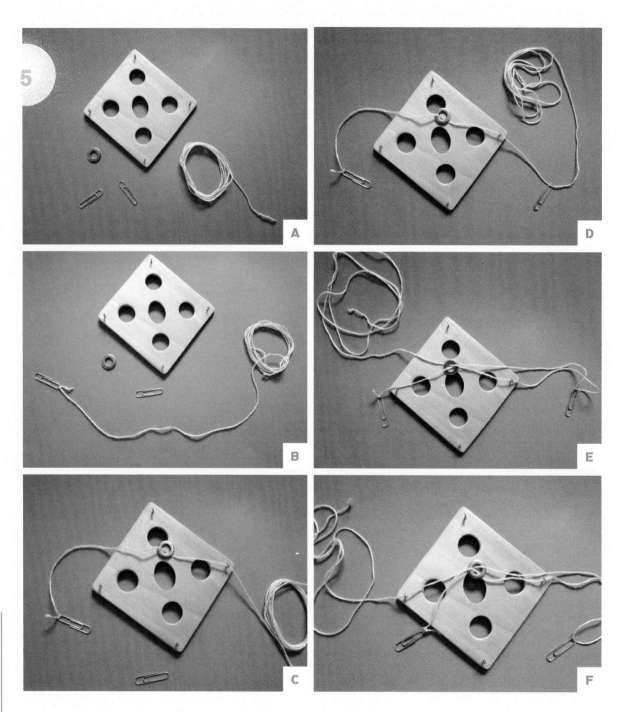

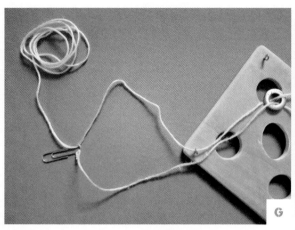 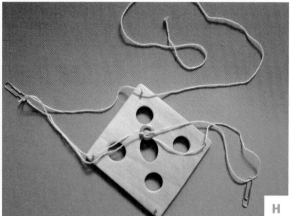

5 **Thread the string (or fishing line) through the screw eyes.** Collect the string (or fishing line), washer, paper clips, and Picavet frame and arrange them as shown (a).

Tie one end of the string to the left paper clip (b).

Thread the free end of the string through the washer and through the right screw eye (c).

Thread the free end of the string through the right paper clip (d)

Thread the free end of the string back through the washer (e).

Thread the free end of the string through the left screw eye (f).

Thread the free end of the string through the first paper clip (the one that has the knot) (g).

Thread the free end of the string through the back screw eye (h).

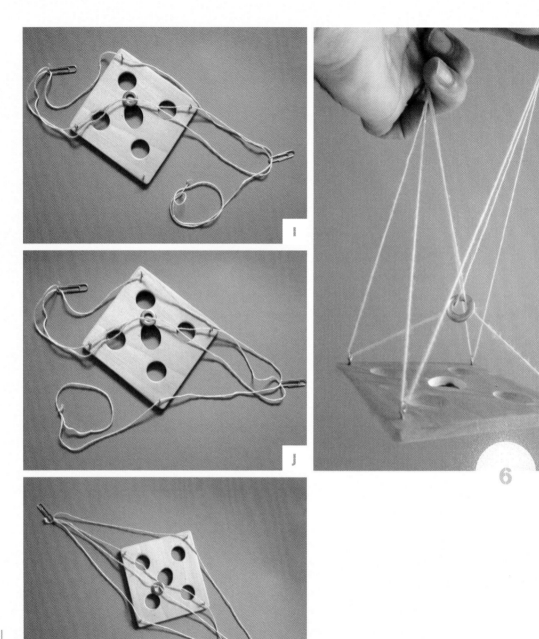

5 (continued)

Thread the free end of the string through the second paper clip (the one without the knot) (i).

Thread the free end of the string through the front screw eye (j).

Tie the free end to the first paper clip. (Now one paper clip will have two knots and the other paper clip won't have any knots.) (k).

6 Adjust the strings so the Picavet is level.

7 **Attach the camera to the Picavet.** Insert the microSD card into the camera. Slide the narrow side of the hairclip through the key ring hole of the camera and snap it into place. Your Picavet is finished.

Note: Store your Picavet in a way that prevents the string from getting tangled. We made a tangle-preventer out of a dowel and a couple of screw eyes, which we use when storing and transporting the Picavet (remove it when you fly the kite).

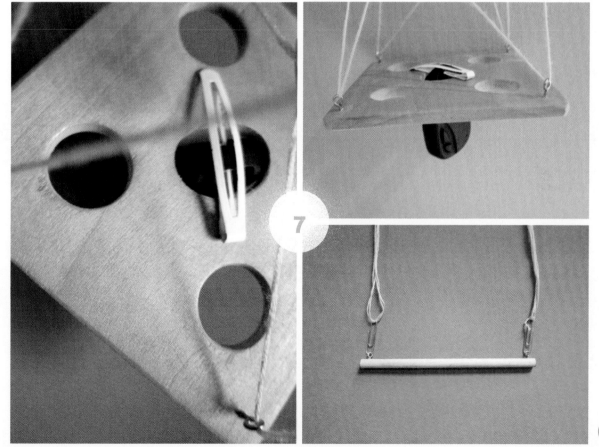

8 **Add looped knots to the kite line.** Tie a looped knot about 8 feet from the free end of the kite line. Tie a second looped knot about 8 inches away from the first one.

9 **Attach the Picavet to the kite line.** When you are outdoors and ready to fly the kite, attach the Picavet to the kite line by sliding the paper clips through the kiteline loops as shown. Wrap masking tape around each paper clip to keep the Picavet from falling off.

10 **Make a video.** Refer to the user manual to turn on the camera and start recording. A 1 GB microSD card will store about 20 minutes of video.

Then fly the kite!

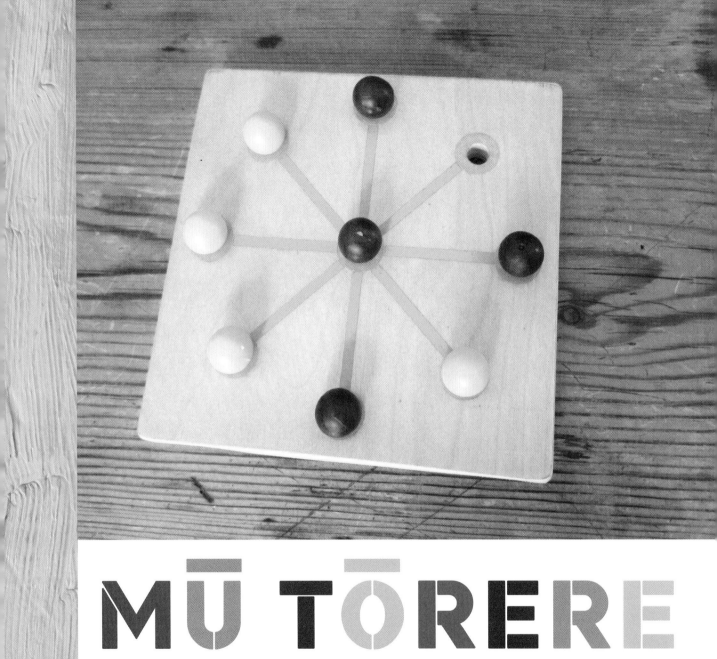

MŪ TŌRERE

An ancient board game of strategy

The Maori people of New Zealand invented the board game Mū Tōrere long before Europeans arrived in the country. According to the New Zealand in History website, European settlers could not beat Maori players at the seemingly simple game, because Maori players could see at least forty moves ahead. Even though my daughters can't see that many moves ahead, they are still able to beat me every time, which infuriates me and delights them.

THINGS YOU NEED TO MAKE A MŪ TŌRERE BOARD

MATERIALS

- **Masking tape**
- **Square piece of plywood,** 5 in. × 5 in.

- **Paintbrushes and paint**
- **Clear acrylic spray**
- **Colored marbles,** 4 of each color

TOOLS

- **Computer and printer**
- **Scissors or craft knife and cutting surface**

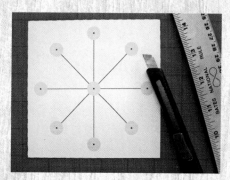

- **Saw,** to cut wood, if needed
- **Pushpin**
- **Pencil**
- **Metal or plastic ruler**
- **Paper clip**
- **Wire cutters**
- **Drill and bits**

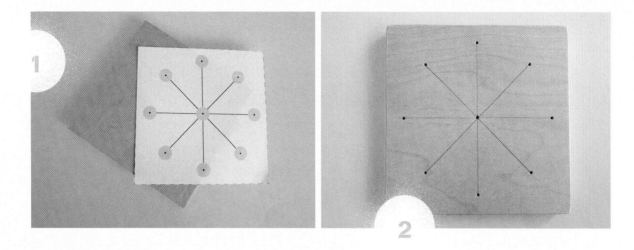

How to Make a Mū Tōrere Board

1 **Print and cut out the template.** Go to makerdad.org and download and print the template. Cut it out with scissors or a craft knife on a cutting surface. Use the masking tape to tape it to the top of your 5-inch square piece of plywood.

2 **Poke pushpin holes into the wood at the nine spots marked on the template.** Draw lines between opposite holes with the pencil and ruler.

3 **Paint the lines between the holes.** Use two pieces of masking tape to create a thin line between two of the holes. Apply paint. When the paint dries, lift the tape and repeat for another pair of holes.

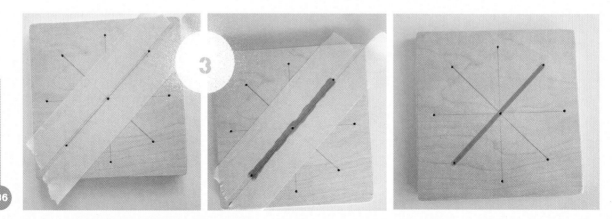

4 **Draw rings around the holes.** Snip off the end of a paper clip with the wire cutters and bend the cut end so that the distance between the bent curves is about ¼ inch. Use it with the pushpin and the pencil as shown to draw ½-inch-diameter holes around each pushpin hole.

0.25"

5 **Drill holes through the pushpin holes.** Our marbles were ½ inch in diameter, and we used a ⁵⁄₁₆-inch drill bit to drill holes through the nine pushpin holes. You can use any size marbles and drill bit you want, but make sure the holes aren't so big that the marbles are hard to remove from the holes.

6 **Paint the circles, using the penciled circles as a guide.** Finish with several coats of acrylic spray.

How to Play Mū Tōrere

1 Place the marbles on the board as shown in Figure 1.

2 Play a round of Rock, Paper, Scissors to determine who goes first.

3 **Take turns moving one of your marbles to any adjacent empty hole.** You are allowed to move your marble to the center hole only if your marble is next to one (or between two) of your opponent's marbles.

4 **If you can't move one of your marbles, you lose.**

Figure 2: Red wins! Figure 3: Red wins! Figure 4: Red wins!

GETTING TO KNOW THE ARDUINO

Learn how to use the popular microcontroller to add interactivity to almost anything

---

The Arduino is an electronic gadget the size of a credit card. You can buy one for about $25. It was invented in Italy as a tool for artists and designers to add electronic interactivity to their projects. In a nutshell, an Arduino does three things:

① It senses the environment. The Arduino has a bunch of *input* pins (they are really holes, but they are called pins). You can attach different kinds of sensors to the Arduino's input pins. For example, there are sensors that can detect and measure the following: temperature, humidity, noise, motion, distance, pressure, light, acceleration, location, radio waves, and oxygen. Think of these sensors like electronic eyes, ears, and other sense organs.

② It processes the information collected by the sensors. The magic of the Arduino is that you can write short computer programs to tell the "effectors" (something that responds to a signal) what to do based on the measurements that the sensors take. For instance, my friend Steve Hoefer built a "secret-knock gumball machine" that uses a sensor to detect the knock-knock pattern someone makes by rapping his or her knuckles on a pad mounted on the gumball machine. If you use the correct knock, the Arduino inside the machine activates a motor that dispenses a gumball. (If you search YouTube for Arduino projects you'll find hundreds of interesting ones.)

③ It makes changes to the environment. The Arduino has a bunch of *output* pins (these, too, are holes that you stick wires in). These output pins can accept different kinds of effectors, such as a light, a buzzer, a speaker, a motor, a heating coil, a servo, and more.

In this chapter, we are going to show you everything you need to know to get started with the Arduino. After you make the examples here, you'll be on your way to creating all kinds of cool electronics gadgets.

MATERIALS

- **Jumper wires,** cut to various lengths
- **Solderless breadboard**
- **3 resistors:** 4.7K ohm resistor (yellow-purple-red), 220 ohm resistor (red-red-brown), 100 ohm resistor (brown-black-brown)
- **LED**
- **Potentiometer, with hookup wire soldered to the leads.** A 1K ohm or 10K ohm will work.
- **Male-to-male header pins,** for servo
- **Servo**
- **Small 8 ohm speaker**
- **Photoresistor**

TOOLS

- **Computer**
- **Arduino board.** There are several different models available. The most popular are the Arduino Uno and the Arduino Duemilanove. Either one will work, and other models may also work with no changes to the instructions below.

- **USB cable,** to power Arduino and upload code. The newest Arduinos use a micro-USB connection, while the older ones use the kind that come with computer printers.
- **30-watt pen-type soldering iron and rosin-core solder**
- **Solder sucker or a spool of desoldering wick,** so you can remove solder easily

How to Conduct Experiments with an Arduino

PART 1: INSTALL AND SET UP THE ARDUINO AND SOFTWARE

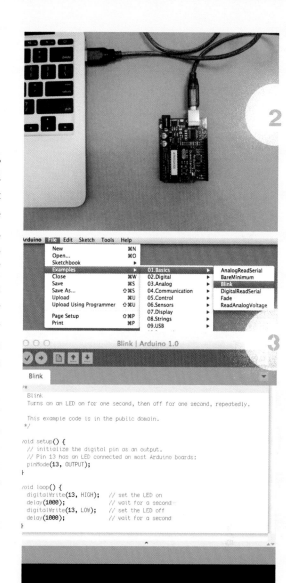

1. **Download the Arduino application (and drivers, if needed).** Before you can use the Arduino, you'll need to download software to your computer that will allow you to write programs and transfer the programs to the Arduino. If you are using a Mac, visit arduino.cc/en/Guide/MacOSX, and if you are using a Windows computer, visit arduino.cc/en/Guide/Windows. These links will provide you with the latest software. (If you are using an older ver-sion of Arduino, such as the Duemilanove or Die-cimila, you will also need to install some additional software called an FTDI driver. Visit the links above to learn how to do this.)

2. **Connect your Arduino to your computer.** Once you've installed the software on your computer, connect the Arduino to the computer using the USB cable. The cable serves two purposes: it supplies power to the Arduino (you'll see a tiny green LED labeled PWR on the Arduino light up when it is on), and it transfers data back and forth from the computer to the Arduino. On Macs, if you are using a newer model of the Arduino, a dialog box will pop up about this new network interface. Click the Network Preferences button, then click Apply. If it returns a "Not Configured" message, don't worry about it. Close the System Preferences utility and move to the next step. The configur-ation is a bit more involved on Windows computers. Visit arduino.cc/en/Guide/Windows for the latest instructions.

3. **Launch the Arduino application.** When the Arduino app loads, under the File menu select Examples, then 01.Basics and then Blink. That will load the program for the first program we will explore.

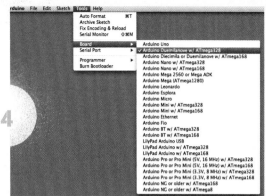

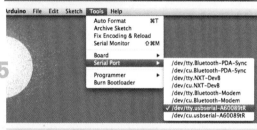

4. **Specify the type of Arduino you're using.** Under the Tools menu, select Board and the name of the Arduino type you've got.

5. **Specify the serial port.** Under the Tools menu, select Board and the name of the serial port. For Macs, it is most likely /dev/tty.usbmodem or /dev/tty.usbserial. For Windows, it's probably COM3, COM4, or higher.

6. **Upload the Blink program to the Arduino.** Click the white arrow at the top of the Arduino application window. It will turn yellow while the Blink program is being transferred from your computer to the Arduino. Once it has finished uploading the program, a small yellow LED labeled L on the Arduino should start blinking on and off once every second. (If it doesn't, go through the above steps again to make sure you have configured your Arduino correctly.)

PART 2: PROJECTS

Make an LED blink

The little yellow LED is connected to the Arduino's digital output pin #13. We are going to use output pin #13 to connect a component LED as a way to get more familiar with the Arduino.

1. **Connect a ground wire between the Arduino and the breadboard.** Use a short jumper wire to connect the GND pin at the top of the Arduino to the ground rail of the solderless breadboard. (For more information about solderless breadboards, see the Friendstrument project on page 132.)

2. **Add a 220 ohm resistor.** We need to use a resistor to prevent too much electricity from going through the LED and burning it out. Connect one lead to digital pin #13, and the other to J18 on the breadboard.

3. **Add the LED.** Connect the short lead (the negative side of the LED) to the ground rail. Connect the long lead to I18.

MARK FRAUENFELDER

194

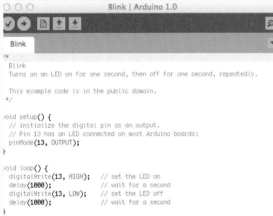

```
Blink | Arduino 1.0

Blink

/*
 Blink
 Turns on an LED on for one second, then off for one second, repeatedly.

 This example code is in the public domain.
 */

void setup() {
  // initialize the digital pin as an output.
  // Pin 13 has an LED connected on most Arduino boards:
  pinMode(13, OUTPUT);
}

void loop() {
  digitalWrite(13, HIGH);   // set the LED on
  delay(1000);              // wait for a second
  digitalWrite(13, LOW);    // set the LED off
  delay(1000);              // wait for a second
}
```

4 **Experiment with the Blink program.** The LED should be blinking on for a second and off for a second (because you loaded the program in part 1; if not, repeat steps 3–6 in part 1). Take a look at the Blink program. We are going to make some changes. Near the bottom you'll see two lines that say "delay(1000)." These lines tell the Arduino to delay from moving to the next line in the program for 1,000 milliseconds (1 second). Try changing one or both of these numbers to 250, then upload the new program again to see what happens.

Note: Arduino programs are called "sketches." We aren't going to explain how to write sketches here. You can instead visit this page at Arduino's official website: arduino.cc/en/Tutorial/HomePage. It offers a good introduction to writing sketches.

Now that you know how to change the blink rate of the LED, let's learn how to do it by turning a knob!

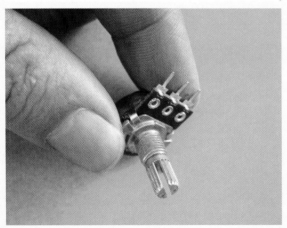

Change the LED's blink rate with a potentiometer

In this experiment, we're going to learn how to control the LED's blink rate with a component called a potentiometer. This is a resistor that is variable. You can adjust the amount of resistance across a potentiometer's leads by turning its metal knob. For this experiment, don't remove the LED and resistor and ground wire you attached in the previous experiment.

1   **Attach the potentiometer to the solderless breadboard.** If your potentiometer has pins that fit into the breadboard, plug them into holes H1, H3, and H5. If it does not have pins, you will have to solder three jumper wires to the three leads. Insert those leads into the same holes (the middle lead of the potentiometer goes into H3).

2   **Attach wires between the Arduino and the breadboard.** Attach a jumper wire from J5 to the ground rail of the breadboard. This will provide a ground connection for the potentiometer. Attach another wire from J1 to the 5V Power pin on the Arduino. Attach a wire from J3 to Analog In pin #0 on the Arduino.

```
                    AnalogInput | Arduino 1.0

    AnalogInput

          example code is in the public domain.

          arduino.cc/en/Tutorial/AnalogInput


int sensorPin = A0;     // select the input pin for the potentiometer
int ledPin = 13;        // select the pin for the LED
int sensorValue = 0;    // variable to store the value coming from the sensor

void setup() {
  // declare the ledPin as an OUTPUT:
  pinMode(ledPin, OUTPUT);
}

void loop() {
  // read the value from the sensor:
  sensorValue = analogRead(sensorPin);
  // turn the ledPin on
  digitalWrite(ledPin, HIGH);
  // stop the program for <sensorValue> milliseconds:
  delay(sensorValue);
  // turn the ledPin off:
  digitalWrite(ledPin, LOW);
  // stop the program for for <sensorValue> milliseconds:
  delay(sensorValue);
}
```

Arduino Duemilanove w/ ATmega328 on /dev/tty.usbserial-A60089tR

3 **Load the AnalogInput sketch.** Under the File menu, select Examples then 1.Analog and then AnalogInput. The sketch will open. Click the circle with the white arrow to upload the sketch to the Arduino. It will take a minute or so to upload. Once that happens, turn the knob of the potentiometer to vary the blink rate of the LED.

Note: Without going into too much detail, let's take a look at how this sketch program works. The middle lead of the potentiometer is connected to Analog In pin #0 of the Arduino. The analogRead() command tells the Arduino to measure the voltage at pin #0. Depending on how far the knob is turned, the voltage at pin #0 can vary between 0 volts and 5 volts. The analogRead() command converts the voltage reading to a number between 0 volts and 5 volts: 0 volts = 0 and 5 volts = 1,023. Other voltages are converted in proportion. This number tells the Arduino the duration of the blink in milliseconds.

Control a servo with a potentiometer

A servo is a special kind of motor that is used in many kinds of machines. Hobbyists use them to make knees and elbow joints in robots, and model airplane builders use them to raise and lower the wing flaps on remote control models. The special thing about a servo is that you can tell it how much to rotate its shaft by sending it a series of electronic pulses. In this experiment, we are going to control the rotation of a servo with a potentiometer.

1 **Keep the potentiometer and the three wires connected to the breadboard.** Remove the LED and resistor and wires leading from them, as we won't be using them.

2 **Insert the header into H10, H11, and H12.**

3 **Insert the servo into the headers.** The black wire goes in H12, red goes in H11, and yellow goes in H10.

4 **Connect a jumper wire between F1 and F11.** This supplies the power to the servo.

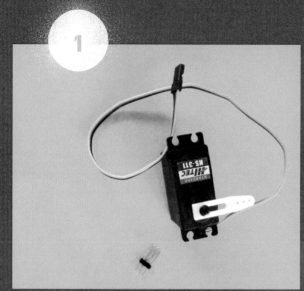

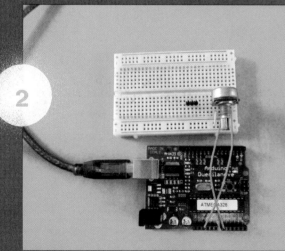

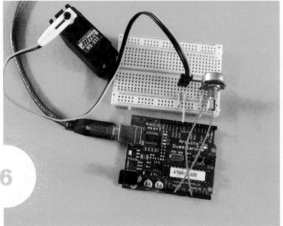

5 Connect a jumper wire between J10 and digital pin #9 on the Arduino. (Note that pin #9 is one of several pins that have the letters *PWN* next to it. It stands for "Pulse Width Modulation," which is the way servos are controlled—with pulses of electricity.)

6 Connect a jumper wire between J12 and the blue-lined ground (-) rail.

7 Connect a jumper between the blue-lined ground rail and the GND pin on the Arduino.

8 **Load the Knob sketch.** Under the File menu, select Examples then Servo then Knob. The sketch will open. Click the circle with the white arrow to upload the sketch to the Arduino. It will take a minute or so to upload. Once that happens, turn the knob of the potentiometer to vary the position of the servo.

Note: This sketch is like the one we used to control the blink rate of the LED. The difference here is that turning the potentiometer knob changes the width of the electrical pulse, which changes the rotational angle of the servo.

Control a speaker tone with a photoresistor

In this experiment, we are going to control the pitch of a tone generated by the Arduino by changing the amount of light falling on a photoresistor. A photoresistor is a bit like a potentiometer, because both allow you to vary their resistance.

1 Remove all the wires and components from the previous experiment.

2 Connect a 100 ohm resistor(brown-black-brown) between J14 and digital pin #9.

3 **Connect the speaker.** The red wire goes in I14 and the black wire goes in the blue-lined ground rail.

4 **Connect the photoresistor.** One lead goes in J20 and the other goes in the red-lined (+) rail.

5 **Connect a jumper wire between I20 and Analog In pin #0.** This pin will measure the voltage that varies as a result of changing the amount of light hitting the photoresistor.

6 Connect a 4.7K ohm resistor (yellow-purple-red) between H20 and the blue-lined ground rail.

7 Connect a jumper wire between the blue-lined ground rail and the GND pin on the Arduino.

8 Connect a jumper wire between the red-lined rail and the 5V Power pin.

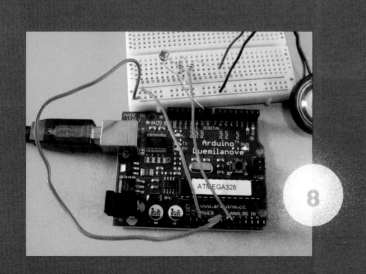

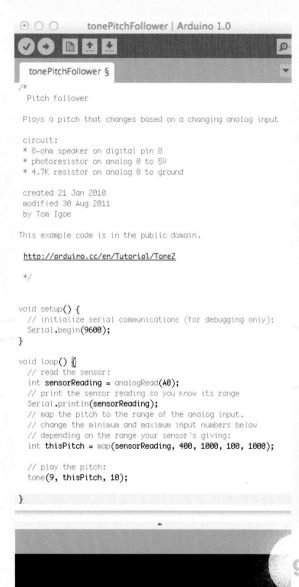

```
tonePitchFollower | Arduino 1.0

tonePitchFollower §

/*
  Pitch follower

  Plays a pitch that changes based on a changing analog input

  circuit:
  * 8-ohm speaker on digital pin 8
  * photoresistor on analog 0 to 5V
  * 4.7K resistor on analog 0 to ground

  created 21 Jan 2010
  modified 30 Aug 2011
  by Tom Igoe

  This example code is in the public domain.

  http://arduino.cc/en/Tutorial/Tone2

*/


void setup() {
  // initialize serial communications (for debugging only):
  Serial.begin(9600);
}

void loop() {
  // read the sensor:
  int sensorReading = analogRead(A0);
  // print the sensor reading so you know its range
  Serial.println(sensorReading);
  // map the pitch to the range of the analog input.
  // change the minimum and maximum input numbers below
  // depending on the range your sensor's giving:
  int thisPitch = map(sensorReading, 400, 1000, 100, 1000);

  // play the pitch:
  tone(9, thisPitch, 10);

}
```

9 **Load the Pitch Follower sketch.** Under the File menu, select Examples then 2.Digital then tonePitchFollower. The sketch will open. Click the circle with the white arrow to upload the sketch to the Arduino. It will take a minute or so to upload. Once that happens, place your finger over the photoresistor and lift it a little to vary the pitch of the speaker.

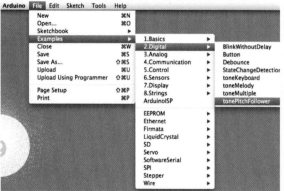

What to try next

These experiments are only the beginning. You can combine the components you have to make something new. See if you can do the following:

1. Control the blink rate of the LED with the photoresistor.

2. Control the speaker tone with the potentiometer.

3. Control the servo with the photoresistor.

Have fun!

"CAN'T LOSE" DICE

A dice game that gives you an unfair advantage

Almost everyone knows the game Rock, Paper, Scissors. Two players face each other and shake their fists to the count of three. On three, each player makes the shape of a rock, a pair of scissors, or a sheet of paper. The winner is determined by the following rules:

1. Rock crushes scissors
2. Scissors cuts paper
3. Paper covers rock

Graphically, the relationship looks like this:

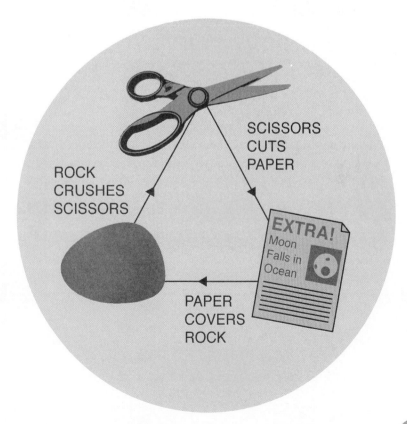

The way to always win in Rock, Paper, Scissors is to wait and see what your friend chooses and then pick whatever object can beat it. But your friend will be able to tell if you cheat that way because of the time delay.

Here's a game that works something like Rock, Paper, Scissors, but you can always win in the long run and your friend will have a hard time figuring out how you did it. Show your friend three colored dice. Point out that they are not like regular dice—they have different numbers on them. Ask her to select one. If she chooses the blue die, you pick purple. Then roll the dice thirty times and keep score. You will almost certainly beat her.

Purple beats blue!

Now give your friend a chance for a rematch. Your friend will probably ask for the purple die, since it beat the blue die. Give it to her and roll the green die against it. You will very probably beat her after thirty rolls.

Green beats purple!

Now your friend will think, "If the purple die beats the blue die, and the green die beats the purple die, then the green die must be the strongest die." She will choose green for the third round. Give it to her and take the blue die. You will likely win most of the thirty rolls.

Blue beats green!

In other words, no matter which of the three dice your friend picks, you can always pick one that will beat it! How is this possible?

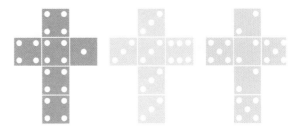

The answer lies in the way the dice are numbered. This particular combination was created by mathematician James Grime.

As you can see, the blue die has 3 on five sides and 6 on the remaining side. The average value of this die is $(3 + 3 + 3 + 3 + 3 + 6) / 6 = 3.5$. If you were to roll this die many times and add up the value of the rolls and divide the total by the number of the rolls, you would get a number close to 3.5.

The green die has three 2s and three 5s. The average value of this die is also 3.5: $(2 + 2 + 2 + 5 + 5 + 5) / 6$.

The purple die has one 1 and five 4s, again for an average value of 3.5: $(1 + 4 + 4 + 4 + 4 + 4) / 6$.

(Interestingly, an ordinary die, which has the numbers 1 through 6, also has an average value of 3.5.)

So why is it that these dice behave the way they do? Let's take a look at all the possible combinations of rolling two dice against each other. With each set of dice, there are 36 different potential outcomes (6 × 6), each being equally possible.

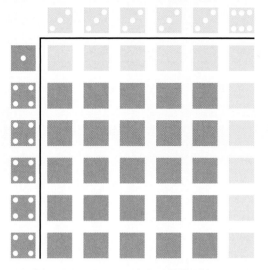

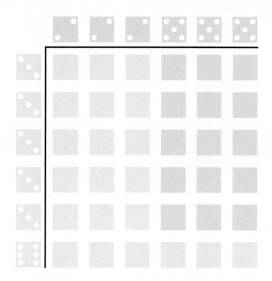

Purple vs. Blue: Of the 36 possibilities, purple wins 25, and blue wins 11. Purple has a $^{25}/_{36}$ chance of winning.

Blue vs. Green: Of the 36 possibilities, blue wins 21, and green wins 15. Blue has a $^{7}/_{12}$ chance of winning.

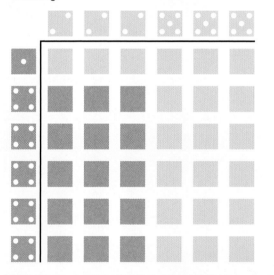

Green vs. Purple: Of the 36 possibilities, green wins 21, and blue wins 15. Green has a $^{7}/_{12}$ chance of winning.

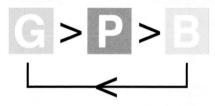

Simply put, no matter which die your friend picks, you can always pick a die that has a better than 50 percent chance of winning. Extra credit: How would an ordinary die do against one of Grime's dice?

How to Make "Can't Lose" Dice

It's easy to make a set of "Can't Lose" Dice. Just get some wooden craft cubes (the same kind used in the Seven-Piece Puzzle Cube project on page 148) and paint them with acrylic paint, adding the white dots according to the layout shown below.

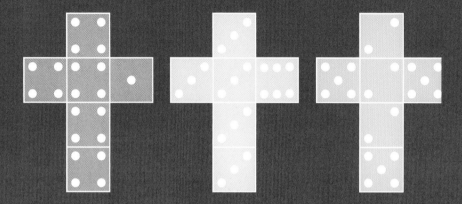

For fun, we wrote a program (using the Python programming language) to see how easy it is to win a game. Download the Python code at makerdad.org and run it on a computer that has Python installed on it. We simulated 1,000 games of 30 rolls and found that the player using the blue die won 778 times and the player with the green die won 222 times. With 1,000 games of 10 rolls per game, blue won 624 times and green won 376 times. And in a simulation of 1,000 games of 1,000 rolls each, blue won every time. Can you explain why this is so?

ACKNOWLEDGMENTS

This book was a joy to create because I was able to spend time with my daughters building the projects in it. Thank you very much, Jane and Sarina, for your help and useful suggestions. I'd also like to thank my original editor, David Moldawer, for working with me on developing the vision for the book, and to his replacement, Katie Salisbury, who took on the project with enthusiasm and a sharp eye. The support and advice from my agent, Byrd Leavell, was outstandingly wonderful, as always.

I would like to thank the following beta testers for trying out the projects in this book and providing us with helpful feedback: Scott Flanders, Allen Downey, Jonathan Bonesteel, Fritz Bogott, Randall P. Girdner, Ken Dashner, and their kids.

I'd like to thank my parents, who are both crafters and makers, for providing inspiration, even though it took decades to incubate in my mind but became incredibly useful in the making of this book.

Finally, I would like to thank my wife, Carla Sinclair, for helping me keep the book on the right course when I veered.

MARK FRAUENFELDER is the founding editor in chief of *MAKE* magazine, the only magazine exclusively devoted to do-it-yourself projects, and the founder of Boing Boing (boingboing.net), a website about cultural curiosities and interesting technologies with 4 million unique viewers each month. He was an editor at *Wired* from 1993 to 1998 and the founding editor of Wired.com. Mark is the author of six other books: *The Happy Mutant Handbook, Mad Professor, The World's Worst, The Computer, Rule the Web,* and *Made by Hand.* He lives in Los Angeles with his wife, Carla Sinclair, and his two daughters, Jane and Sarina.